Prescription For A Successful Life

The Complete Guide For A Fulfilled Life In Every Domain

Revised Edition

Jean Daniel François, M.D.

Also by Dr. Jean Daniel François:

Les Clés de la Réussite Authentique (in French)
Prescription for an Exciting Love Life
Prescription for a Successful Career in Medicine

You may visit the author's website:

WWW.SUCCESSFULLIFE.US

Or you may e-mail him at:

JFRANC6704@GMAIL.COM

G.O.A.L. Inc.
1713-19 Ralph Avenue
Brooklyn, NY 11236
Phone: 718-531-6100, Fax: 718-531-2329

Printed in the United States of America
Revised Edition
Cover's concept and design : Denise Gibson
ISBN: 978-0-9823142-3-4

For information or to order additional books or
for any other reasons, please write:

Jean Daniel François, M.D.
P.O. Box 360543
Brooklyn, NY 11236
U.S.A.
718-531-6100

WWW.SUCCESSFULLIFE.US

He that is over-cautious will accomplish little.
~Johann Friedrich Von Schiller, 1759

Excerpts of What People are Saying About

Prescription For A Successful Life...

"Yes, we can. YES I CAN!!!

"The *Prescription for a Successful Life* by Jean Daniel François contains a series of essays that add up to a life philosophy; what you need to know: essentials for 'Every Aspect of Life.' In earlier times many people kept the Bible at the Center of their life.

"Dr. François' book is a most helpful, practical addition to the important messages of the bible for all of us, the young, the old, men and women. In a series of chapters ranging from financial success to love, from health to spirituality his book is a guide everyone can use for the success we SHOULD be striving for: a balance and harmony that leads to success and the proud feeling, 'I did it.' Dr. François challenges us to change. He talks about the new you.

"In chapter 1 Dr. François makes clear his view that success can only be measured within one's own individual value system. He defines the core of success as knowing your own desires and identity and your commitment to them. It is not a materialistic commitment; it is a commitment to yourself.

"His book is especially timely now that the United States has a President whose direct origins are African. President Obama calls for a change in our society. The change Dr. François challenges us to pursue is inner change, change of an individual. He makes us aware of the importance of an inner conviction, of taking individual responsibility for our affairs as the key to a successful life. (is this the definition of success?)

"The chapter on women's success is reflecting on women's increasing influence weight in the workplace and foremost in society is most welcome. One could almost say now in a positive sense: *'cherchez la femme'* if you want to understand a successful life for woman, in a group of professionals, in and out of the home, among men and husband and children. ...

"His essays speak to all of us. Many of us are refugees from small countries and from non-English cultures and we may feel at times the difficulty of being accepted... not perhaps on 'racial' grounds. Prejudice is not linked to race alone.

"Using examples, Dr. François makes us aware of the many divisions in society, along various lines, race, culture and education. His examples juxtapose the responsibility of an executive to employees, to make us better understand the dilemma of a black executive and his or her black staff. Always the emphasis is on the individual responsibility of making good decisions.

"His examples and advice address personal and practical matters as well. In chapter 3 for instance, he gives practical advice for success in matters such as buying a car, refinancing your mortgage... Dr. François takes a no nonsense approach to success.

"He gives especially valuable discussion and advice on the responsibility of the black minority for its own success, an advice however that is valid for all of us. The emphasis is on YES I CAN. Each and every one of us..."

~ Ivan Bodis-Wollner M.D., D.Sc.
Professor of Neurology and Ophthalmology
Director, Parkinson's Disease and Related Disorders Clinic,
Center of Excellence, in Brooklyn, NY

Comments About the First Edition

"Finally, here is a book that has something for everyone. No one can take the time to read this book thoroughly and not feel the urge to make a change in his or her life…"

~Anthony Benoit

"More than a self-help book…this is a practical non-judgmental book of observations and advice. After reading, it is obvious the author has spent a lifetime observing human nature. He is sharing his experiences and studies with us by distilling complex and deep ideas to their essence. His thoughtful observations have been gathered into this complex, yet easy to read book. Dr. François' book really is a gift of knowledge that any reader will be sure to take away something and apply it to their own personal growth. This makes it an easy, almost compelling book to read and re-read passages and make notes in the margins. Too many books of this type are dogmatic or of narrow vision. The author, out of compassion and not ego, seems compelled to want to share his insights as a way to 'give-back' to us readers. Although you sense many accomplishments and successes in his own life, a clear modesty emerges and you never feel lectured to. *The No Nonsense Approach to a Successful Life* has something for everyone, no matter what stage in their own personal growth they find themselves. Truly inspirational without being maudlin."

~Seeker of Knowledge "Den", NY

"… Successful Life" motivates you to take control of your life. It offers you practical ideas on how to position yourself to be successful in anything you set your mind to accomplish. It also provides you with insight on how to develop better relationships with others. No matter what stage of life you are at, you can make positive Changes and move forward to become a better you and be of service to society"

~ P. Cole, Ohio

"I felt empowered after reading *The No-Nonsense Approach to a Successful Life* by Jean Daniel François. I had never read a self-help book before and don't feel I need to read another one because this book was so complete yet very concise; it truly was the essentials for every aspect of life. Three convictions of the author which rang true in me were: success is accessible to **all**; there are **infinite** ways to be successful and a **holistic** approach to success is most beneficial. I recommend this book to anyone; it promotes serious contemplation. Every individual must define their own life and what would make it successful. Never does François suggest that if you blindly follow in his footsteps you will be a great success. Instead he gives you guidelines to fit your life (no matter what it is). François acknowledges the inevitable pitfalls, roadblocks and other difficulties that come during life's journey and presents ways to recover from them and get back on the success track."

~ Rosetta M. Gibson "Book Club", NY

Acknowledgements

A legion of people aided me in the writing of this book. Some read the manuscript; others spent long hours making comments and giving me precious advice. I am indebted to all of you.

This Book is dedicated to all the men and women who never give up but continue to fight to improve their conditions in every domain. I tip my hat to you all. Many thanks to each and every one of you.

Disclaimer:

This book does not intend to replace the role of any expert or competent professional to assist in securing an accomplished life. It does not guarantee the satisfaction of anyone in his or her quest to succeed. It is another approach to remind the readers or to highlight ideas that can benefit, educate an astute reader who is seriously engaged in the journey for a successful life. The author shall not be held responsible or judged liable to anyone or institution for any loss, disappointment or damage attributed directly or indirectly by the ideas expressed in this book. Any examples, any names used do not represent any specific existing or defunct individuals or institutions. Feel free to inform us of any error that may have inadvertently slipped in. Thanks!

Preface To The Revised Edition

It is highly gratifying when a writer receives encouraging words from readers of every walk of life. It is even more exciting when it is the first publication. I am very grateful for the letters, phone calls and warm greetings received after this collection of essays was first published under the title *The No Nonsense Approach To A Successful Life*. The suggestions and comments are well appreciated. Having a book that addresses *success* with the intention to suit everyone's needs is definitely a challenging task. Because people are different and their needs are diverse and limitless, defining success requires meticulous analysis, clear vision, adequate knowledge of what everyone really wants in various aspects of life. Nevertheless, all of us can agree that we need a dynamic and fulfilling life. This is a serious matter. The old views and approaches have become obsolete. As the global community is getting more sophisticated, the path to success becomes more difficult. But, if the world is full of hardship, we need to remember that every crisis brings along new opportunities. New concepts, better knowledge are now required for an ever changing environment. The word success also needs to be revisited in order to reflect the advances in technologies and scientific discoveries that revolutionize the planet. It is time for a holistic view of success. It should have a personal meaning in various aspects of one's life, free of pressures and fears. The best antidote for failure is the ability to learn from any mistakes, and to move forward regardless of the challenges. Adversities must serve as a stepping stone towards reaching the designated goal. The ideas that people read in this book spring from observation and personal experience. They underline the importance of individual daily effort and commitment to move forward and reach the set dreams. When the winds start blowing in the wrong direction, you need solid structures to stay the course. It is my sincere hope that people from all backgrounds, all ages, all races and all orientations will find in this book enough inspiration, motivation and education to meet any challenge, overcome all adversities in order to have a better life. Please do not just read the following pages, take notes, underline some ideas, shake your head and then return to what you are conditioned and accustomed to do. This time you must take the decision to act upon those ideas and monitor the results. Of course, my approach may not be agreeable to all; feel free to make the necessary adjustments. But I believe it is a worthy endeavor for many who are troubled, and are seeking encouragement and ideas to get out of the bottomless pit of hopelessness

As you know, regardless of its content, no book can be written without the help of altruistic, dedicated friends and family members. To all of them I want to express my sincere and deepest thanks.

Enough say! Let us pull up our sleeves and start working at it! Good luck!

From The Preface To The First Edition

"Not again! Not another book about success!"

Maybe that's what you thought when you saw the title of this book. And you are right. In our culture, we are constantly bombarded by the word *success*. Because success is an interminable topic, and it is also an integral part of our daily dreams, many people feel compelled to shed light on the subject. People's opinions of success generally fall into two categories: There are those who believe *it will never happen for me*, and then there are those who say *I can't deal with this right now!* Our culture and values encourage such automatic reactions. This book challenges your acceptance of the status quo. Most of us are willing to read about the few who have made it. We admire them; we have their pictures in our walls and we buy their products. Some of us may even envy them for a moment. Then we go back to our daily routine. We are so busy running, working, huffing and puffing for our daily bread that we don't have time to think about our work towards our own success. But it does not have to be this way. Life was never intended to be like this. Success is accessible to all. The key difference between this book and other books about attaining success is that in this book I want to engage you on the road to success and stay on this road with you. I want you to experience the ascending levels of a better life because you can. We can reach for the stars together. Start living your own success stories instead of reading stories about others who have made it. After all, whether you actively participate in life or not, life continues its course. So you may as well do something about it. Give it your best shot!

In recent years the world has made great strides in a variety of areas, and more technological, scientific and educational progress is expected going forward. Although technology has made the world smaller, people feel more and more distant from each other. We are living in a strange and alien world. Everyone is busy trying to cope with a demanding and bewildering life. Why is this so? What can we do about this? Can we change it? Invest some time in reading this book; you are bound to take a new and improved approach to life. We are in this arena called life together, and giving up is not an option. Despair leads to destruction. The fight is hard, the obstacles are monumental, but you can overcome them. It is not enough to say *I want a successful life*. You must be motivated, disciplined, vigilant, and persevering. And most of all, you must have a game plan.

This book's underlying themes recur throughout. To press on despite the many obstacles you may face, you need guidance; you need to remain resilient; and you need to be observant—in all areas of life. You need to make use of all your talents, coupled with dedication and hard work. You need a source of motivation to develop a better relationship with your surroundings and to develop coping mechanisms for difficulties and challenges. This book will help you on your way to a successful life.

I sincerely hope the chapters that follow will inspire you to discover a proactive life, uncover your boundless potential, and reach all of your goals. Let us combine our energy to embark on this journey together, and reach the other side safely. The time has come to experience lasting changes that ensure a better and more enjoyable life for us all.

Prescription For A Successful Life

The Complete Guide For A Fulfilled Life In Every Domain

Revised Edition

Jean Daniel François, M.D.

Table of Contents

What Is A Successful Life?

Why are we here on this earth? Why do we exist? Where do we come from? Where are we going? Is there a reason for human life on this planet? What role— if any—do we play in the universe? These questions and many more have been raised throughout centuries. They have baffled the greatest thinkers, writers, historians, archeologists, religious leaders and philosophers through ages. Many answers have been provided. But they do not seem to satisfy everyone. One fact remains: Generations have gone and gone; life is short; we need to be practical.

The beginning of all of our various endeavors on this earth stem from the reality that we are alive. Once an individual's light is extinguished, that person's life ceases to exist. So it makes sense to define the concept of life itself. For our purposes, let's consider life to be the sentient period between birth and death, especially when we can make choices and decide on our own what to do and what to avoid. It is the aggregate of vital phenomena characterized by growth, reproduction, adaptation, movement, organization, etc. It is defined in relationship to the different functions that distinguish living beings from inorganic matter. Regardless of your age, race, sex, beliefs, or location on this planet, there is a minimum of activities required for life to be worth living. To stay alive and choose to maintain a meaningful existence of your own free will, you first have to ensure that you take care of primary needs—that you breathe, eat, sleep, drink, and excrete. Unfortunately, too many people never go beyond this bare minimum of life requirements. For various reasons, they never have a chance to reach their full potential. Some do not dare to dream or have hope. They have no opportunity to see or even think of a better tomorrow.

According to United Nations statistics, millions of people go to bed hungry every night. More than 6 million children under the age of five die each year from malnutrition, and 1.2 billion people worldwide live on less than a dollar a day. In many instances, these circumstances have been passed on from generation to generation. When the economy goes sour, the impact is felt globally and the situation gets even worse. In the western hemisphere, we can at least see and hear through the media about those who live an abundant life. Not only can we dream, but we also can forge our destiny and turn it into the very existence we desire. No one owes us anything. We must take charge, be in control of our life, and make the most of what we have. We are responsible for every decision we make.

We live in a world where no one seems willing to accept blame; this hampers our growth in all domains. If you are a mature person, you acknowledge your role in every situation. Accept your mistakes, learn from them, and determine to do better next time. If you want to lead a successful life, you must stop the blame game, the grudges, the bitterness, and the excuses.

Everyone has a personal definition of life. Everyone has a distinct course of existence, marked by a series of events, activities, and expectations. The different factors that mold each individual life (socioeconomic and cultural background, for instance) not only affect your behavior, but they also determine your expectations. People define *life* many ways:

- "A life is the sum of all your choices." *Albert Camus*
- "Life is a promise; fulfill it." *Mother Theresa*
- Life is the aggregate of a series of commitments and expectations.
- Life is a game.
- Life is a lonesome road.
- Life is hell.
- Life is a marathon.
- Life is a school.
- Life is a constant struggle.
- Life is a gift, a journey.
- Life is a garden of flowers.
- Life is a delicate rose.

…and on and on…

Overall, life is the most precious gift bestowed upon mankind. We must make the most out of it. Our actions reflect our projection of life; therefore it is important for every one of us to come up with our own definition of life. This reflects who we are, where we come from, and what we expect to accomplish throughout our existence. The primary factors in leading a successful life are to be alive, have a positive attitude, enjoy every moment of our existence, and appreciate it as a special privilege that must be cherished, nourished, and protected. To put it bluntly, "Life is action!"

Definition of a Successful Life

At one time or another, most everyone questions the purpose of their own existence, and we have all heard different variations on the dictum, *"A life without purpose is a waste." The word purpose is defined as the reason for which one exists with the end result in view. It requires: goal, perspective, need, decision, action, choices, strategies, knowledge, support system, motivation, self awareness and mental health. Without purpose, life is meaningless, boring, and a total waste. Please bear in mind the facts that: a.) everyone is created for a purpose; b.) everyone is required to find that purpose and pursue it.*

Shakespeare compared life to a stage on which every individual is a character with different scenes to play. Upon the opening of the curtains, you begin to act out your assigned role. Then, at an undisclosed time, you must leave. When that moment arises, you must go, no matter what. Although some believe that this is only a temporary exit, you have to make the proper use of your allocated time on this earth. Life cannot be passive; you must allocate some time to tailor your definition of life, so that it fits your individual needs. As you come up with your own definition of a successful life, you must identify your priorities and take the necessary steps to achieve your goals.

For one person, a successful life may mean the ability to maintain a close relationship with a divine power. For someone else, success could mean having a loving family. Yet another person may define success in terms of money and material possessions. Whatever your definition of success, you can accomplish it; yet it is up to you to do so. As an exercise, write down your own definition of success in your own words. Why is it essential to write down your own definition of success? First, as a mature human being, you know your needs better than anyone. Second, this exercise allows you to stay focused as you make positive steps toward accomplishing your goals. Third, and most important, this exercise limits the impulse to blame others for outcomes in your life, as it forces you alone to decide on your goals.

Naturally, each of us has suffered misfortunes, mistakes, and disadvantages. The challenge is to overcome these inconveniences. William H. Johnson said, "If it is to be, it is up to me." Neither your government, nor your parents, nor your children, nor your friends, nor your enemies can decide your success. It is all up to you!

Peyton Conway March, observed that there are "three things we crave most in life—happiness, freedom, and peace of mind." As you struggle in your daily life, make a note of your chief concerns and expectations. The most common answers include security, stability, freedom, and peace of mind. If you analyze the question even further, you can probably compile the response in one word: *happiness*. As a matter of fact, most of us need all of the aforementioned conditions to be happy. Conwey March said it's a law of nature that happiness, freedom, and peace of mind "are always attained by giving them to someone else." Accordingly, the true definition of a successful life must not only include individual goals, but must also include the concept of relationships. The human approach to relationships is played out in two dimensions: vertical relationship, which entails the rapport between the person and the supernatural; and horizontal relationships, between individuals. Any authentic definition of a successful life must not only include the ability to reach goals and satisfy personal needs, but also it must include spirituality and fellowship with others. This is a dynamic process.

As you look around, you can identify five groups of people:

1. Those who expect nothing, care about nothing, and drudge through their lives on a day-to-day, hand-to-mouth basis.

2. Those who are consumed by selfish desire, covetousness, anger, and want. They strive to satisfy these desires by any means necessary. They are often envious and angry, and they expect others to meet their needs.

3. Those who want to be successful. They talk about it day and night. They even have it all figured out on paper. Unfortunately they never take the necessary actions to make it a reality.

4. Those who know what they want expect a lot out of life, are willing to work hard to reach their goals, yet do not know how. They buy into the common belief that success is reserved for a lucky few.

5. Those who believe that they are like eaglets, developing their keen eyesight and majestic soaring flight. They believe that with the proper perspective and circumstances, it is only a matter of time before they start to fly high. These people have their goals set and are determined to take action in order to reach them.

The first step toward a successful life is an unbiased determination of which category you belong in. That you are reading this book shows that you are

not waiting to be hand fed, nor are you the type
to be envious or jealous or to just talk about it.

To make the best use of the advice in this book, you
need to *first find* a clean and quiet space to concentrate,
a cozy spot away from most distractions. Use this time
to search deep inside of yourself and discover what is
lacking in your life. What is it that you want more than
anything else? What is it that you are prepared to devote
the rest of your life to doing, even if you are not paid to
do it? In short, what is your purpose on this earth? You
owe it to yourself to be truthful, to stop procrastinating,
and to stop hoping that somehow, as if by magic, things
will work out fine. It is time to end that reactive life and
begin a proactive one. This is a defining moment; it is
an obligatory passageway that helps you to discover the
reason for your existence. Once you find that reason,
you feel brand new and life becomes meaningful. You
have something to look forward to and work toward.

Someone has said to you, "You are your own worst
enemy." You cannot let that define you. You need to
have the confidence to make your dreams come true.
Stay focused, and above all stay the course. You have
to be aware of—and able to sort through—other
people's discouraging words and unsolicited ill-advice.
At one time or another, we have all been prey to the
negative words of an acquaintance, a friend, or even
a family member. In order to shield yourself from
such negativity, you must take the necessary steps
to make changes to improve your support base.

A dictionary definition of success is "the attainment of
fame, wealth, or power." But simply expressed, success
is based on the ability to reach the desired goals and

get the expected results. According to Earl Nightingale, "Success is the progressive realization of a worthy goal or objective." It is an individual call. You are not here to carry the load of the entire world; your own load is certainly heavy enough, and if you handle it courageously, you will make a difference. You are not here to live vicariously through others and see your success through the eyeglasses of your next-door neighbors or coworkers. You must identify what you really need to accomplish in life. This is an individual engagement and a vital cornerstone. It takes time, inspiration, perspiration, and preparation. What you want depends on who you are. Man is a complex and a complicated being. You have to find your own specific definition of a successful life, narrow it down, and be able not only to see the ultimate goal, but also to plan each step toward it.

An adolescent wanted to be a preacher. As time went by, her desire to reach her goal got stronger and stronger. She graduated from high school and went on to college. Her parents, advisors, friends, and roommates all told her it was a foolish idea. She was very bright, she had many talents, and she was advised to go after what would guarantee a more secure and respectable life. She finally went along with their plan. She spent four years in college and two years in medical school. She eventually quit school and got a regular job. Luckily, some common sense found its way into her brain, and she went back to what she originally wanted. She became a happy preacher. She is not rich, but she is content because she was able to pursue her dream.

You often meet people who have gone through a lot of effort, time, energy, and financial difficulties to reach their goals. After all of the time, gray matter, and energy invested, many discover that their initial desire is not what they really wanted; yet they have invested so much in the endeavor that they refuse to change gears. They go through the motions frustrated, disappointed, miserable, and even angry. This is why you have to be convinced of your dreams without any outside pressure. You may need guidance, but you must be allowed to make the final decision.

Deciding to read this book means you have chosen, if only subconsciously, to lead a successful life. The *next step* is to create a detailed description of what you want in that successful life you have chosen to live. Remember that determination, assiduousness, and discipline can even compensate for lack of talent. You cannot compromise or sell yourself short.

Many people do not even try to improve their lives. The most common reasons for a stagnant life include: 1–fear of failure, 2–anxiety about change, 3–unwillingness to face required challenges and obligations that go with such a decision, 4–concerns about what others may think or say, and 5–flashbacks from previous failed experiences.

You need to look beyond what ordinary people see. Place your choices into perspective with the various spheres of life: spiritual—moral, personal—familial, professional (career, entrepreneurship, education, etc.), financial, social, emotional—mental, and health.

How will these different choices enable you to grow closer to your beliefs, values, and convictions? After you write everything down, you must determine the measurable steps and the period in which you plan to accomplish your goals. Throughout the process, there may be the background noise of skepticism repeating softly to your subconscious: Is it possible? Can I really make it? What if I fail? What about my past failures? The remedy for the background noise of self-doubt is determination, faith, motivation, perseverance, and the ability to replace negative thoughts with positive ones.

When you are convinced, dedicated, and committed, you can expect the best because you really deserve the best. Those who make it start by believing, and then they act decisively. It is worth it to start behaving today as you wish your life to be in the future.

When I was a young man, I got my first job as a part-time messenger. When I went to work, I was always dressed in a suit and tie. The other messengers used to make fun of me, by calling me "the boss." It never bothered me, because in my mind I knew I was an eagle temporarily refueling among the chickens. Sure enough, after bidding for a few higher positions, six months later I got a promotion to junior accounting clerk and I left the rest of them behind.

It is not enough to dream of being successful. You must not only work toward this dream; you must behave like your dream will come true, or better yet, act as if it already has come true. Sometimes it is worth making a leap, even when you do not have everything completely figured out beforehand. You may feel as if you are jumping out of an airplane without a parachute. Trust your gut and stay with your main dream.

Do not allow your fears to get the better of you. If you are consumed by fears, all hell will break loose. Fears are often fantasies that play on your emotions to keep you bound to them. A great majority of people are unhappy with their jobs. Many won't even look for a better one because they fear losing what they already have. They settle for less and live miserably for the rest of their lives.

Remember this however: If there is no risk, there is no success. You must, of course, be wise, practical, and knowledgeable. But to dare to risk, to work hard, and have patience and perseverance is to dare to succeed. If you do not believe in yourself, who else will? If you don't take yourself seriously, who will? If you do not work hard enough toward your goals, who will? The choice is yours.

Every challenge brings along an opportunity to overcome it. It is better to face each challenge than it is to stay idle or to hide while wishing things will somehow just disappear. They will not! You can't just go around saying, "I want to be successful!" This does not mean much to your brain. But if you say, "I want to be a millionaire!" a dialogue immediately starts within you. You begin to envision your life as a millionaire. You ask yourself questions: How? When? Can I? Can I not? An internal argument sparks.

If you say, "I want to be a millionaire in five years!" you visualize the thought, you act like the thought is true, and the intensity of the dialogue increases. Your brain is making the appropriate adaptation. I am presenting you with these examples in order to show you that you must make your goals specific and state them clearly.

If you keep feeding your subconscious with great ideas, your horizon broadens and your mind stays focused on great things that you must act upon. It pays to be assertive, constructive, positive, and direct. You have to use your common sense, review your objectives regularly, repeat them, visualize them, and feel them.

The brain cannot clearly differentiate between fact and fiction. Thus, your brain has the ability to filter in what matches your beliefs, aspirations, and goals from the billions of pieces of information that bombard it daily. Pictures trigger faster and more lasting stimulation than words ("a picture is worth a thousand words"). You need to cultivate the ability to visualize for yourself the way you want your life to be six months, twelve months, two years, and five years down the road. If you do this visualization, you will be surprised by the impact it has on your life, as it can dramatically elevate your moods and aspirations.

Your goals must be big enough to allow you to expand to your maximum potential without making you explode into tiny pieces. They must be practical enough so that if you do not attain them, you won't get depressed or discouraged. You must be pragmatic. Buy a notebook, a Palm Pilot, or whatever will help you to stay organized, to write down your inspirations, ideas, and dreams as you go along. You need to have a Plan A and a Plan B. Remember, prioritize your objectives and stay the course. When should you start? Now! Every second of every day is precious. From now on, every one of your thoughts and activities must be geared toward your objectives.

It is often lonely on the road to success. But once you get there, you will find plenty of people to hang out with. You may have instances of frustration, rejection, defeat, mockery, resistance, and inconvenience, but you should not make these times harder than they are. You should not try to reinvent existing wheels. You should make use of the available resources that can contribute to your dreams. You should take advantage of qualified mentors.

In summary, you are apt to live a successful life. The key depends on your choices, your motivation, and your discipline. If you have a set of objectives, and you understand what is really at stake, you can reject the easy alternatives, persevere, and be on your way to achieving the life you want. Once you commit yourself to a goal, you must accept the entire process of attaining that goal; consistent with your moral and ethical values, of course (the end cannot justify immoral means). You must review your plans at each stage of the process; if an adjustment is needed, you must consider the options that will facilitate your journey to success.

There is not one uniform, magical, quick way to succeed. But there are general rules followed by those who have made it. Let's look at a sketch of a successful person. Generally, successful people are not cynical and manic workaholics without a minute to breathe. They are not bossy and lazy people who expect everyone else to support them. They do not spend their time dreaming of living in a flowery bed of ease and praise. They are instead well-balanced people, who know how to manage their time and engage in many different activities. Because everyone's needs and desires are different, it may be inappropriate to decide for everyone on the planet where and when to reach a given objective. But you must make progress and periodically analyze your progress to make your objectives into realities.

The Stages of Success

Here are the steps to achieve success:

1. Know who you are. Take a sincere and honest inventory of your present circumstances.

2. Decide what you need and be convinced of this need.

3. Believe that change is possible. It is your responsibility to do the necessary planning.

4. Determine the appropriate steps and resources and pass them into action.

5. Develop appropriate coping mechanisms for facing obstacles.

6. Evaluate and measure progress, making any necessary adjustments.

7. Fight procrastination and the urge for instant gratification.

8. Persevere; continue the struggle with discipline until victory is yours.

9. Be passionate and follow your dreams.

10. Get under the wing of a qualified mentor and develop the ability to relate to others.

You must keep yourself in check as you move forward. Take into consideration your environment, personal beliefs, and the necessity to be realistic, without settling for the easy way out.

Those who live in a successful world go through three stages:

1. The induction period.

2. The stabilization period.

3. A lifetime of success.

The Induction Period

You are tired of going through the same routine while the situation goes from bad to worse. You vacillate between wanting to give up and wanting to fight. An intense argument brews from within. You begin to take inventory. First, you evaluate your weaknesses. You believe you need to change course; you are scared, but deep inside you know you have to take some risks and make some changes. You follow your gut instincts. You free yourself from your fears, and you decide that it is worth taking a chance. This induction phase allows you to test your choices, acquire information and knowledge, adjust your schedule, weigh your pros and cons, and begin to measure the results of each change.

Liz is a single mother of a preteen boy. She has been working as a clerk in her neighborhood for ten years. Her minimum wage position includes long hours, no sick days, no health coverage, and barely any holidays. To top it all off, she receives no recognition for her work, and her boss is obnoxious. She is ambivalent about the entire situation, yet she is scared to even ask for a raise. Several other employees have left because of the work environment, and they have told Liz that they are doing well. A former coworker called to inform her of an opening in a new office with a boss the friend doesn't know. The first three months is probationary, at fifty percent more than Liz is making now. If she gets through the probationary period successfully, the salary jumps to twice as much as her current one. But if things don't work out, Liz will be laid off and will be eligible for unemployment. The permanent position also includes employee benefits

*and the opportunity to go to school and have the company
pay for her tuition. The only inconvenience is that it is
an hour away from her home. What should Liz do?*

The first thing she must do is to send her résumé to
the company while she weighs the risks and benefits
of her choices. She has to take into consideration the
traveling distance, her preteen child, her sick mother, her
salary, and her career. Her entire life is passing in front
of her. This new job will bring her more money, with
room for advancement and the opportunity to further
her education, but it requires more traveling time and
will leave her with less time with her child and her sick
mother. And there's a risk she'll end up without any job.
When she realizes all of this, she is in her induction phase.
The induction phase should not last long. Although it
requires changes and choices, it should take only a few
days or weeks. Some complete this phase slowly and
adjust accordingly. Others make a drastic, precipitate
break with their past and embrace a brand new way of
living. The decision to continue the same old way of
living may kill all enthusiasm and dim all motivation. Liz
could decide to stay put because she likes being close to
her family and she has been able to tolerate her lousy job
and lousy boss all this time, and she may reasonably fear
being laid off from her new job. She might ask for a raise
at her current job, although she may not get it. She may
even get fired or laid off just for asking and be forced to
look for another job. That really would make her see the
light. It is an individual decision. But complacency and
indecisiveness may make her go with the status quo.

The Stabilization Period

Congratulations! You have taken a giant step toward transforming your destiny. You have been inducted into the Hall of Successful People. Unlike most induction ceremonies, in which you are honored for what you did in the past, induction into the Hall of Successful People honors you for what you are going to do in the future. You determine the privileges attached to such a rank. At this stage of the game, you must remember two things:

- Always remain in control and fully committed to following your dreams.

- Do not let circumstances torpedo your plan; instead, use your circumstances to pursue your goals.

You are now ready. All your activities are geared toward the goals you have set for yourself. You can no longer play around; you cannot afford to be pulled in a thousand directions because of friends, family, cultural stereotypes, salespeople, or the media. There is no time for destructive, hazardous, non-productive activities. There is no time for nostalgia, or crying, over the way things used to be. Life is dynamic. You are already engaged, you are in the middle of the ocean, you can only move forward. You know what you want. You are moving along toward your targeted objectives. You are aware of the roads to avoid and those to travel: only those that lead to the real goals. Not every so-called opportunity will help you or fit into your plan. You know how to take maximum advantage of your time.

George is a physician who has some issues with a few licensed car repair shops, so he usually chooses to repair his car himself. He discovers that his car has an engine problem, and he weighs his choices. Is it worth spending his entire weekend trying to figure out the situation and then determine whether or not he can fix it? Or, should he take it to a licensed mechanic's well-equipped shop while remaining focused on what he is good at, being a doctor? Obviously, reason will tell George to stick to his expertise.

Remember, you are now a member of the successful people's club. This is where you get and give support to stay the course, where you function in the most efficient way by reviewing your goals daily, measuring your progress, and making the appropriate adjustments.

Lifetime Success

As a member of the Hall of Successful People, you have committed yourself to a lifetime of a successful lifestyle. This includes seeking increased knowledge; being involved with the community; being useful to others; achieving social, cultural, and spiritual fulfillment; as well as working toward your legacy.

The ultimate, long-term goals for success are individually tailored. This is why you need to set the goals as high as possible, yet reachable; otherwise you may limit yourself, lock yourself in a box, or even become bored. Boredom can lead to frustration, carelessness, and laziness. Proverbs 24 says: "Go ahead and take your nap; go ahead and sleep. Fold your hands and rest awhile, but while you are asleep, poverty will attack you like an armed robber."

Life's success is achieving the specific goals that you initially set for yourself. Further steps depend on your resiliency, comfort zone, overall well-being, and ability to keep going after more and more challenges. This is why I advise that you enjoy life while pursuing your goals. This is a sure way to make it pleasant to continue while you welcome other perspectives and venture toward other horizons. If your path is continuously strenuous and painful, you cannot last for long. Look at popular crash diets. At the very beginning, it is usually a crisis or a near-crisis that triggers the desire to change. But no one can go on with so much deprivation for long, and so these diets always fail in the end.

It is a Friday afternoon. Larry's manager calls and tells him that he appreciates his great contribution to the company; however, because of financial constraints, he has to let him go. He shakes Larry's hand and wishes him all the best. After a restless night, Larry wakes up the following morning with a lot of bills to pay—credit cards, rent, tuition, utilities—and his wife is in the third trimester of her third pregnancy. Suddenly, there is no income. This definitely puts Larry in a bind. He must act quickly. Once he recovers from the shock, he must deal with reality. He must not only start changing his approach and start knocking on doors for a new job, but he also must start seeing things through a broader perspective.

The decision to take appropriate steps to reverse a given situation or bring change in your life is always commendable. However, to remain successful, you must broaden your scope to encompass all the spheres of life. After all, you cannot be successful by compartmentalizing your life, by deciding to change here and not change there.

Peter has worked hard all of his life. He has noticed that the harder he works, the tougher his overall situation becomes. Finally, because of some unexpected event, some personal encounter, some news, or because he has read this book, he realizes that things cannot go on like this forever. He decides to take control of his financial situation, and he puts his house in order.

The commonsense approach tells him to

- Look at his total income and its various sources.
- Consider his list of expenses to see what is absolutely, positively necessary and what can be eliminated.
- Make a comparison.
- Address the negative balance and find ways to bring about a positive change.

Certainly he is going to write down a few options, including finding another job, acquiring more knowledge and becoming better educated, doing more overtime, getting a raise, cutting down or eliminating expenses (movies, theater, expensive lunches, impulse buying); and then he can make a proper decision he can stick with. To make it through these challenges requires self-control, discipline, and perseverance. The successful outcome depends not only on the given (sometimes painful) triggering factors or the urgent catalysts for change, but also on other aspects of life, including character, level of maturity, education, culture, and peer pressure. Everyone who chooses to succeed has the responsibility to deal with various aspects of life; including the physical, emotional, psychosocial, intellectual, spiritual, and professional aspects. Success requires a structural framework to stand on, based on your goals, conditions, moral values, and abilities.

Seven Main Obstacles to Success

1. Poor self-image, emotional incontinence and instability.
2. Resistance to change, intolerance to criticism,

discounting weaknesses or hiding behind them or blaming others.

3. Procrastination / lack of discipline.

4. Fear of failure and failure to stay the course.

5. Lack of knowledge / preparation.

6. Failure to be kind, grateful and humble, but becoming complaisant and arrogant.

7. Confusing success with happiness.

1. Poor Self-Image, Emotional Incontinence and Instability.

If you have no self-respect, low self esteem and little regard for yourself, it will be hard to appreciate your worth and know what you deserve. This requires honesty and maturity. If you are unstable, unpredictable, and labile, or if you constantly change your mind about your goals, the road to success will be more difficult. Past conflicts and baggage must be resolved before you take off toward your objectives.

2. Resistance To Change, Intolerance to Criticism, Discounting Weaknesses or Hiding Behind Them or Blaming Others.

Nobody is perfect; nobody can please everyone all the time. To make it in this life, you have to accept criticism. Address the issue, make the appropriate adjustments, and move on. You know it already: Change is the only constant in life. Your obligation is to evaluate the changes that occur and the impact they will have on your dream. You need to be fair enough to know your shortcomings, and make provisions to muffle them—if unable to get rid of them all. Be mature enough to recognize where you fail and learn from your mistakes. Avoid blaming others, especially when it is your fault.

3. Procrastination and Lack of Discipline.

Because of the fragility and brevity of life, it is fair to analyze, take inventory, and weigh the options. But there is a time to decide to get on with it. You cannot indefinitely agonize over every little detail. Life is short and time goes by rapidly.

4. Fear of Failure and Failure To Stay the Course.

After you decide to strive for success, you are guaranteed to encounter challenges from many sources. Adjustments are called for. But do not panic; this is why the emphasis is on choices, planning, and engagement. Do not try to change course at every single wind that blows your way.

When she was a baby, one of my children was always ahead of her milestones. She started taking steps when many infants in her age group were just crawling. She was doing exceptionally well and was constantly stimulated to strive for more and more. When I came in the door one evening, she was very excited to see her dad. In her rush to come and meet me, she unfortunately made a misstep and took a big fall. She became overwhelmed with fear and did not take another step until she was almost two years old.

Fear of falling or of failing can paralyze you and make you miss some key opportunities that could otherwise make a world of difference in your life. Fortunately for my daughter, she caught up. But as an adult, it is hard to catch up. Some opportunities may not come back your way for a long time.

5. Lack of Knowledge and Preparation.

No one knows everything about anything. Certain areas of your endeavor may bump against your lack of knowledge and expertise. This is why research and homework are important. You must be willing to seek help when you need it.

6. Failure to Be Kind, Grateful and Humble, But Becoming Complaisant and Arrogant.

Generally, it is easier to cope with adversity then to deal appropriately with great success. There have been many instances when the media point out the other side of some famous people with their reprehensible behavior. It is paramount to stay vigilant when things are going your way; and to remain gracious, polite, and nice to others. All of us must remember that the pathway to success is not forged alone. Many people and circumstances have contributed to help you get where you are. It is easier to come down than to go up and stay up. Life is unpredictable. The current blue sky and sunny day do not eliminate the possibility of a dark and tempestuous turn around. Therefore, it is worth remaining kind, grateful and humble

7. Confusing Success With Happiness.

Success is being able to achieve a set of goals. Happiness is a state of mind. A clear example: The chief executive officer of a large company is a successful person, by virtue of attaining the goal of becoming a CEO, whether or not the company ends up doing well. But the CEO, whose long work hours often put a tremendous strain on family relationships, is not necessarily a happy person.

The Core Principles For Success

- **Your personal identity.**
  Know yourself as much as is humanly possible.

- **Your degree of commitment to succeed**
  Have purpose, passion, hope, and determination.

- **Your approach to and philosophy of a successful life.**
  Strive for something more meaningful than materialistic accumulation of wealth.

- **Your true motivation to succeed.**
  Your motivation should be to serve others and leave a legacy for the betterment of mankind.

Desire for Successful Changes	Score	Action to Be Taken
Full satisfaction with current situation	0	None
Mild desire to change	1—2	Monitor situation
Moderate desire to change	3—5	Seek motivation
Substantial desire to change	6—8	Take inventory
Strong desire to change	9—10	Start now

It's your call. Make it now

The New You: A Call to Change

Tom was born in a small town and he grew up in a big family. Because of financial challenges, everybody in his family was always working two to three jobs to make ends meet. Tom's grandfather played a key role in his upbringing. He was always there for him, and he was a conscientious, hard worker who was constantly thriving. One early Sunday morning in late autumn, the leaves were falling off the trees under a light and intermittent rain, as Tom's grandpa sat in his usual chair.

Tom said, "Grandpa, when are you going to retire?"

Tom's grandfather was a bit taken off guard, and to Tom's surprise he said, "Sonny, life is like the sky. It can be clear, blue and sunny now then suddenly it becomes cloudy and rainy. You must make the most of what is available. Life is like a ship on the ocean. Sometime the wind will be in your favor, sometime it won't be. You need to know where you are going and adjust based on the conditions beyond your control. Life is a journey on the highway. You must keep driving, while making sure you enjoy the ride. The moment you stop, you run the risk of being run over. You start tumbling down a slippery slope where you might never recover."

Unfortunately, after a satisfying life, Grandpa had to go. After his grandfather's death, Tom decided that he wanted to become a physician because of an unfounded belief that his grandpa died from lack of care. He wanted to make a difference in the lives of all those who would come to him for care.

As Tom grew up, he had to fend off challenges from all directions. He had a lot of responsibilities. Caught in the daily exigencies of life, he gave up his initial goal. For many years, Tom was an average worker dragging the heavy cross of shattered dreams; he was too consumed by remorse and debt to take stock of himself. Day in and day out, he tried his best to smile.

One day, while sitting at an end-of-the-year social gathering, a youngster came out of nowhere, tapped him on his shoulder, and said, "Excuse me, sir, are you a doctor?"

Tom said, "No, I am not!" and the kid went on his way. But Tom agonized over the question. He suddenly felt lightheaded, with palpitations and nausea; he was sweating; he needed some air. Tom left discreetly and drove the twenty miles home like an automaton, for the little boy's question kept repeating in his mind, the sound track to scenes from his childhood.

"Are you a doctor?" As he voiced the question aloud, an argument started within him. One side of him was assailing him with questions that the other part of him never had a chance to answer convincingly. He realized he was settling for less and selling himself short. That night he decided to change course. He decided to go to medical school, to which he was accepted after his thirty-fifth birthday. And in spite of his age and the obstacles that he had to face, he studied and fulfilled his dream.

Everyone is in control of his own destiny. You may face various challenges and hurdles on your road toward fulfilling your dreams, adversities may pave your way of living. But do not give up. Persevere, sooner or later you will find the right formula, discover the proper solution, put the puzzle together, and create the right recipe that will move you toward your success. The burning questions remain: Have you been fortunate enough to identify the passion of your lifetime? Have you discovered what you enjoy and value on this earth, what you would do joyfully regardless of the difficult circumstances? Have you discovered what you are great at? What goals have you set for your life? What price are you willing to pay? How far are you willing to go? What are you willing to forego? What sacrifices are you willing to make? Are you willing to go the extra mile? Do you just freeze or give up somewhere along the line, even when you are just about to finish the course? When you know that most people want to succeed and improve their conditions, you must ask yourself what it is that makes you different. What makes you go for the top, while the others vegetate at the bottom? Are there people who are born to succeed while others just sit back, letting life pass them by? Or are we all hardwired to make it, but some of us are too afraid of failing, of running into difficulties, of being ridiculed by others to even try?

There is a special aura surrounding those who are successful or who are bound to succeed. They constantly need to thrive. They have an everlasting thrust to go for more. Some people are just more ambitious than others, aggressively outperforming them. Recall the story of Jacob in the Bible. Jacob came out of his mother's womb holding the heel of his older twin brother as if to tell him, "Step back, and get out of my way, for I am going to outdo you." The rest of the story stands for itself. In order to make it, it is not enough to have a set of goals. You want to have a great and prosperous life, but that is not enough. It takes other elements: energy, patience, determination, persistence, tenacity, perseverance, ambition, zest, and enthusiasm. But where do these qualities come from? Are they genetic or gender-based? Or are they based on external circumstances, such as the level of stimulation during infancy, family upbringing, teachers, education, communities, culture, religious beliefs, and deterministic factors? Or is there just the appetite to succeed? The jury is still out. Nevertheless, you should not be surprised if the anthropologists, psychologists, sociologists, and neuroscientists come up with an answer that is a combination of all the above. Regardless of what the answer is, we know that it is possible to make a choice from the initial example at the beginning of this chapter. Tom took it upon himself to return to his childhood dream of becoming a doctor. By giving up the current conditions of his life, he took a risk to go after his dream. One of the key steps to succeeding in this life is to make active choices and be willing to create change. It is time to look deep inside of you, listen to your inner voice, listen to your heart and brain; extract the essence of your destiny and bring it out in the open. You know you have gotten it out when you feel relieved. Then join all the dots together. Voila! You become full of zest, energize and ready to go and conquer in order to get your reserved spot under the sun.

Benjamin Franklin said it: "Nothing is certain but death and taxes." I say that one more thing is certain: We are all subject to change. The only way for our present life to be acceptable while we press on toward a promising future is to be committed to change. To dream is to change, to grow is to change, to acquire knowledge is to change, to apply acquired knowledge is to change, to gain experience is to change, to decide is to change; all in all, our species lives by going through changes. President John F. Kennedy said, "Change is the law of life. And those who look only to the past or present are certain to miss the future."

Choose to Change

You know now that change is inevitable. You should assess the components that are pivotal to the specific changes in your life. You can either sit back and let fate dictate your life or you can take action by making the appropriate choices and discover the inner purpose of your existence in this world. Your choices depend on who you are. To choose actively means you realize you are in charge of your destiny and you are responsible for your choices. To make such a decision requires that you first define yourself, you are aware of the realities of life, and you find ways to reconcile dreams and realities.

Who am I? Who are you? Who are we? Various factors combine into making you and me who we are. Our parents, family structure, genetic complement, peer influence, education, teachers, socio-cultural environment, beliefs, values, choices, health condition, personality, community, city, and country all play a role in determining who we are.

Inherited Package

Parents

Your parents or guardians, their beliefs, values, political and racial views, vices, professions, and general approach to life, all have affected who you are today. Parents play a vital role in the success of their offspring. Such a delicate task begins even before conception.

Parents set the example for the way their children see the world and act in it. They are role models, for good or bad. Generally, children get off to a good start if their parents are respectable figures with disciplined, goal-oriented values, and good diligent habits. During the early years, children love to imitate the examples they see. They can initiate and complete some tasks themselves with their parents' encouragement. Actions always speak louder than words. The good examples that parents set transmit a loud and clear message and provide an exemplary path to follow. If children choose a different pathway, if they decide to yield to peer pressures and engage in reprehensible activities, the parents at least can be at peace with themselves because they did their best. Conservative parenting teaches kids that there is a price to pay for every choice; it also creates responsible citizens who learn early in life how to appreciate what they have. Parents who follow these guidelines motivate their offspring to improve their status and do better than their forebears.

Well-balanced, friendly environments represent a milieu conducive to better results in life. But many people strive for excellence even though they grew up in a dysfunctional family. This raises the question as to whether or not other factors influence our development.

Genetic heritage

Besides the impact of your immediate parents through the way you were brought up, you have another strong inherited component: your genetic heritage. Children look more or less like their parents. How often do we hear things like, "She has her mother's eyes"—or height, temperament, talents, weight, etc.? These declarations are a testament to the fact that parents transmit biological traits to their offspring through genes.

Human beings are a diverse species, with ample external variations. Studies of identical twins reared apart show that inherited genes will pursue us, no matter how we are brought up. Children inherit a range of characteristics and preferences from their parents. Everyone has a genetic constitution and exhibits certain traits or inherited qualities. Genetic vulnerability, behavior, intelligence, nervous system quality, certain illnesses, and other characteristics can be traced from parents to offspring.

Environment

Like genetics, the environment plays a key role in human health and development. Environmental factors that shape your destiny include your schooling (private or public, the institution's academic strengths, class size, and available technology) and the type of community you grew up in (urban, suburban, or rural, and the pace of life there). These are contributing factors in the making of who you are. A child who grows up impoverished in a big city with a dysfunctional family is less likely to adopt the appropriate behavior and thinking patterns for success. Yet, despite the odds, it is still possible for such a child to make it. Some roads are more tortuous and more perilous than others, but people still make it through.

Individual Package

Personal assessment for change

Inherited factors can facilitate or hamper your ability to gather speed toward your success. But the ultimate decision is up to you. Success is a package. There is a direct relationship between the different spheres and degrees of success and your core self-determination to reach your identified goals. This is why it is absolutely necessary to know yourself, to know your weaknesses and your strengths, so that you can capitalize on your strengths and minimize your weaknesses.

Ms. F.C. is tired of her past and present life. She has made the conscious decision to change; but she has a specific weakness. Since her childhood she has had a tendency to be rebellious, to disregard law and order, and to ignore basic safety rules. She has poor impulse control, and as a result of this she was involved in a couple of unnecessary brawls. Therefore, despite her determination and her resolution to change, she may need to see an expert in personality disorders to help her cope with her problem.

If you have a pertinent physical impairment or illness, you need to seek treatment to be able to function to your maximum potential. In other words, there should be no stone left unturned to put you in your best shape to go for your goals. If certain factors in your life, such as your education, job training, lifestyle, psychosocial behavior, budgeting abilities, and family setting, need to change, make a plan to fix what needs to be fixed. If there are specific triggers that may hamper your motivation or coping skills, identify them and deal with them immediately. If you are stuck in an abusive relationship or if you have any addictions, these issues must be addressed. Otherwise, there will be perpetual cycles of self-defeating behavior. You need to pause and reflect on your personal life history. Evaluate your current quality of life— marital status, family structure, support network, ability to function, education, employment, income, personal habits, medical and mental conditions. Identify previous goals that you set in the past. Evaluate those you reached, as well as those you didn't. Analyze why you were able to attain the former and why you fell short of the latter.

Pay attention to your appearance and behavioral patterns; be able to change and improve what is changeable and improvable: the odor of alcohol consumption or of smoking, personal hygiene, attire, speech patterns, tone of voice, vocabulary, general demeanor, interaction with others, temperament, thought processes, and eating habits.

Some of these are easier than others for any individual. The main thing is to do your best, based on the circumstances. Review all of these factors. You must have an unwavering willingness, readiness, and commitment to change. You must understand your current condition, evaluate the consequences of change, and know the price you must pay for such a choice. Once you set the goals and know the expectations, you must start immediately. If you are bound to succeed, you must undergo a renewing of the mind and a change of heart.

The brain plays a key role in making appropriate choices and changing your mood. Watch for what is coming into and being stored inside the brain. I keep a constant watch on my thoughts and all ideas, avenues, or sources that can affect my thoughts. I refuse to dwell on negative ideas, bad news, or anything that may obstruct my progress toward a meaningful, positive life. I have spent too much time already on what is bad, what I cannot or should not do, or what is too late to change. Now I have to stay focused on good things. When bad things happen (as they will), I deal with them immediately and move on.

The journey to success encompasses the choices made and the acceptance of change. In order to change, you must define yourself. The factors that define you include biological, familial, social, cultural, environmental, and governmental components.

The role of habits

From childhood to adulthood, we learn many things that establish the disposition of our character. Through learning and repetition, we develop a fixed pattern of behavior that becomes automatic. Once the brain has stored the pathways of some given pattern, we act as if on autopilot, seemingly without effort. This is what we call habit—"another us," our "second nature." Habit is relatively stable and molds our lives in various domains.

More often than we desire, we acquire bad habits along with the good ones. It is not easy to get rid of these bad habits. Scientists and philosophers have offered techniques to help us develop stronger and more rewarding habits to replace the bad ones. These techniques include the use of certain patterns of intellectual behavior or habits of mind (discussion, dialogue, communication, perspective, analysis, imagination …). It takes one habit to replace another.

Once we decide to be successful, we must decide to form new and good habits; we must keep repeating the new choices over and over. We must imitate good examples and progressively learn to establish a new way of life. Through conviction, determination, practice, adaptation, repetition, self-awareness, concentration, and motivation, sooner or later the appropriate choices should become automatic, like reflexes.

Human beings are born to be successful. Our habits play a key role in attaining success. The key is to eliminate the bad habits, replace them with good habits, stay focused, keep a clear perspective, and keep a close watch on what you feed your mind, your character, and your environment.

Reasons—why you will live a successful life

You will succeed because:

- You are aware of the opportunities available.
- You decide to set attainable goals.
- You believe in yourself and your ability to make it.
- You take the necessary steps toward making your dreams into realities (short and long term).
- You have the skills and abilities to execute those steps and reach those dreams.
- You accept changes and you are willing to be the active driver of change.
- You have a reasonable time table while fleeing procrastination.
- You have chosen good habits.
- You have developed appropriate coping mechanism when facing inevitable challenges.
- You find time to measure progress and adjust accordingly.
- You resist the urge of complaisance, you refuse instant gratification.
- You are disciplined, perseverant and passionate about your dreams.
- You remember to enjoy life throughout the process.
- You have put yourself under the wings of a trust worthy mentor.

I recommended making a list of short-term and long-term goals. Decide what you can accomplish in six months to four years. Imagine your life as effectively changed and start living your life as if it already has.

Once you have reached such a dimension, you must be aware of possible distractions, such as fear, negativity, and rejection by others. These are the trials and difficulties of life.

Eight Ways To Sustain Positive Change

1. Have Faith.

After you take the necessary steps and express the desire for change, you must have enough faith in yourself, your vision, your decisions, your energy, and your available resources to engage in your new life. Previous failures are nothing but stepping-stones to jump ahead. You need to believe in the community and the society in which you live. Hopefully you will be so committed and determined that you will begin to share the dream with others. Your antennae are well tuned to capture any opportunity waves that pass within your radius. Your radar is always on for new and improved ways to help you progress.

One snowy Sunday morning, Danny ran into the house to ask his dad for a bike. Although it was strange for a kid to be thinking about a bike in the middle of winter, after a short pause, Danny's dad told him that he would buy it in the spring. Shortly after, Danny was making all the sounds of the bike, as if he were actually riding it in the middle of winter. In his head it was spring or summer, and he was on the street passing by pedestrians; he was blowing his horn, telling them to clear the way. As if that were not enough, later on his sister Sarah complained to their dad that Danny would not let her touch his bike. You get the picture! Children have faith; they know how to live their dreams until they reach the time when the facts of life makes them change into only picturing reality. When you have a dream, you need to make your subconscious mind see it and start living it.

2.   Keep Records, Be Organized.

To stay the course, you need to document your path and remember the initial inventory of your condition. Write down the good decisions and capitalize on them, record the bad decisions to learn from them and avoid repeating them in the future. Take a look at your surroundings. Review the lists of your friends, acquaintances, places you go and things you do routinely. Be courageous enough to keep only those that are positive and beneficial to your personal growth. Regularly review your written goals and your personal mission statement to see how you are progressing. If you are not on target, remember to make the necessary adjustments.

3.   Learn And Know.

As you are cruising along, you may discover your mistakes, your shortcomings; do not panic, and do not turn back. You must face them, seek knowledge, do your homework, educate yourself, get trained, find a mentor, ask, consult, learn, and apply the acquired knowledge. Experience proves that people are happy to help, if there is something in it for them. If you want it all, you may keep it small. If you want it big, with careful discernment, share it!

4.   Challenge Your Fears.

Many times things go well until you become so self-conscious that you panic, get scared, and become paralyzed by your fears. Fear is an innate emotion that challenges your survival. As you embark on your quest for a better life, apprehension, ambivalence, and doubt form a tapestry of concerns that may cross your mind. The worst thing that can happen is that you fail. You already realize that each mistake provides an opportunity to gain experience for success. So you need to be bold, trust your judgment, and focus on your expectations. When you trust your gut feelings, you can dive in to what you really want to do and what you believe you can do.

5. Be Disciplined.

Dot your i's and cross your t's. As you move forward, you need to be careful to have good documentation and finish every task you start. If you just keep starting new projects, you may never finish any of them. It is better to make a list of what you want to do, put the list in an order that makes sense, and work through it one item at a time. Broaden your ways, means, and resources. Don't confuse yourself with a superhero. You can only be in one place at a time, and you can only do one thing at a time. You should not spread yourself too thin and risk an irreparable tear. You need to be responsible and compliant; adhere to your set goals.

6. Put Aside Time For You.

Many successful people try to keep going non-stop. There may be some who can do that successfully, but most people who try end up burning out. The wise approach is to take time to "smell the roses." You need to take time for yourself. Change your pace or change your scenery. Listen to your inner self and savor what you have already accomplished. Appreciate your gifts, talents, and assets without becoming arrogant, flashy, or intolerable. Taking a break can protect you from exhaustion and from feeling overwhelmed. A breather may give you new insight or inspire you to try new approaches. Avoid the compulsion to pursue many objectives at the expense of your social life or your health. Remember, success is not a drug intended to provide euphoria. It is not an instant or magical life change. It is a package and a lifelong process. So you must enjoy life as time progresses.

7.   Be Patient.

Rome wasn't built in a day. Learn patience and perseverance on the road to success. Our written history is full of the names of people who stuck with their goals and plans. How many more people failed to make a mark because they were too impatient or did not persevere? Napoleon Hill, in his book *Think and Grow Rich*, relates a compelling story about the Darbys, who stopped drilling only three feet away from one of the richest gold mines in Colorado. When you review your goals and assess your progress, you must be careful not to be blindly and naively optimistic or careless; nor should you be extremely pessimistic or exigent. You have to be well balanced, keep your boundaries in check. Use your judgment and even seek help if necessary. Patience and perseverance will lead you to victory.

8.   Beware Of Obstacles.

As you are sailing along, sooner or later, trials and tribulations will head your way. You must expect them and be prepared to bypass them or deal with them without getting depressed or spinning out of control. As you look at the transformation of a caterpillar into a butterfly, let it be an inspiration to keep on striving for a sustained course of success.

By now I hope you recognize your own desire to morph and change from a caterpillar into a butterfly. The butterfly will of course never be a caterpillar again. So should it be with you!

Contrast Between the Old You and the New You

Old You	New You
Shortsighted	With renewed intelligence
Lacking knowledge or having limited knowledge	Well-versed and eager to know more
Rash, careless, and lazy	Committed, responsible, decisive
Following the crowd	Knowing where to go and how to get there
Wishy-washy and indecisive	Positive, decisive, and goal-oriented
Unstable or having low self-esteem	Stable and highly motivated
Envious, jealous, and angry	Calm, cool, and collected
Focused on weaknesses and problems	Focused on strengths and solutions
Having a negative attitude	Having a positive attitude
Expecting instant gratification	Awaiting delayed gratification

You must strip the old you to assume and embrace the new you.

Sixteen Key Questions For the Successful Person to Answer

All of us would like a better life. Here is your checklist for success.

1. Are you the successful type?

2. Can you remember five tasks that you successfully completed in the last two to five years?

3. Are you dissatisfied with your current condition?

4. Do you accept the fact that you can do better in all areas of your life?

5. Are you really willing to change?

6. Do you really understand the costs and the benefits of change?

7. Are you aware of the possible obstacles, and can you cope with the trials and inevitable difficulties that go along with change?

8. Do you know your strengths and weaknesses?

9. Can you handle criticism?

10. Can you forgive yourself when you make mistakes?

11. Do you know where you want to be in six months, one year, and five years?

12. Do you have a detailed plan for where you want to be and when and how to get there?

13. Are you willing to adhere to your set goals and prepare yourself to meet the challenges?

14. Can you review your goals frequently and make adjustments accordingly?

15. Are you willing to seek all the needed resources to make things work for you?

16. Can you appreciate and enjoy each step of your success?

Human Success, Your Individual and Financial Success

Key Steps For Human Success

The road to success is not the same for everyone. Your goals and the steps you take to reach them play a pivotal part in your climb to the top. You need a progressive and determined will. In no particular order, here are thirteen keys that make it easier to ascend:

- Life, time, and health
- Choice
- Attitude
- Motivation
- Maturity
- Forgiveness
- Friendship
- Discipline
- Action
- Religious belief
- Gratitude
- Authenticity
- Manners

Life, time, and health

Obviously you need to be alive to succeed.

Life is not defined as an aggregation of a number of years, but according to the way you use your allotted time. Everything gravitates around time. If the world offers you everything it has without the proper time to enjoy it, such an offer is a mockery.

A day contains twenty-four hours for all. The difference is in how each person uses these hours. For example, how much time do you spend in bed, watching television, working, or having fun? The key is to do the maximum within the minimum amount of time possible. Time never stands idle waiting for us. You must always fight not to waste time. You must orient yourself according to your priorities, while being very efficient. A life spent in inertia, hesitation, and blame is not an option for those who want to succeed. When you have life, time, and health, success depends on the choices you make, the way you use your freedom, your circumstances, and the events that affect your life.

Choice

Your life is limited. But your desires, your dreams, and your wish list are limitless. The key is to find the right formula to reconcile infinite wants with limited resources. It all depends on your choices and your priorities. Here are ten factors that must govern your choices for success:

1. Have clear and precise objectives.
2. Take inventory: do the proper analysis, establish your needs by order of priority, and categorize them as short-term or long-term.
3. Objectively identify your potential. Seek the advice of others if need be.
4. Have faith in your ability to succeed.
5. Identify and capitalize on the ways, the means,

the alternatives, and the strengths. Minimize and avoid the weaknesses.

6. Set a solid foundation, an unshakable base, from which you can reach to the sky.

7. Act with enthusiasm, confidence, and determination.

8. Review your results regularly.

9. Be willing to adjust, accommodate, and change accordingly to reach your goal.

10. Find time to enjoy life without being pompous and presumptuous.

Your success depends on your will and the path you take. And your freedom is limited only by your choices and your actions.

Attitude

You meet many different kinds of people in your life. Sometimes you run into those who are full of energy, and you wonder if they are from the same planet as you. After a closer look, you realize that they too face challenges and problems. And they are under the same amount of pressure and stress as you. One word makes a world of difference: attitude! Attitude is your psychological disposition, a proactive way to approach life. It is a personal predetermination not to let anything or anyone take control of your life or manipulate your mood. Attitude allows you to anticipate, excuse, forgive, and forget, without being naïve or stupid. It is a personal decision to stay in control and not lose your temper. Attitude provides safe conduct through all kinds of storms. It helps you to get up every morning happy and determined to get the most out of a brand new day. Whatever happens—good or bad—the proper attitude makes the difference. It may not always be easy to have a positive attitude; nevertheless, you need to remember you can face a kind or cruel world based on your perception and your actions. You can change and improve your attitude at any time. Why not start today?

Motivation

Motivation has been a key to the success of every great man and woman in history. Motivation feeds the unwavering will to pursue a goal at any cost. It allows you to ignore all previous statistics, silence all considerations, and put aside even prudence to go after one objective: success! With motivation, nothing can stop your unswerving decision to reach your goal. Motivation allows you to learn from the past and exploit the present, while remaining focused on the future.

I was the first of nine children. Many times I had to go to school twice a day and return home on an empty stomach. (This was during the days and a in a place where there were no food programs in schools.) When the church bells rang at seven in the evening, my brothers and sisters and I looked at each other and realized that once again our beloved and diligent mother could not find anything for us to eat. Usually, she would add salt to the pot of beans that she agonized over for hours. Then she would give some to each of us while repeating proudly, "Remember, you are gold. And gold is always precious, even in the midst of mud." If by some bit of good fortune some sugar was found in the house, we improvised lemonade at a ratio of one liter of water per spoon of sugar and a piece of lemon. All of us took some and left some for the following morning, just in case there was nothing to eat the following day.

Even when I left the house to study, it was a challenge because of regular and long blackouts. Sometimes I studied in the street while my mother kept watchful eye on us all. When it was too late or we had to stay inside for some other reason, I had only a small gas lamp.

Today, I can eat more or less where I choose. During a visit to Europe, my family and I were eating at a high-class restaurant. I suddenly realized that even though I was eating the best dishes prepared by renowned chefs, I did not feel one fifth of the pleasure that I felt with my little bowl of salted beans. How do you explain the huge discrepancy between the youngster who could not satisfy his hunger, and the man who lives well today? One word makes the difference: motivation! During those dark moments of my life, I knew that my choice was either to succeed or die. I knew that I was in charge of my success or my failures. Motivation goes a long way!

Maturity

To succeed in this life you must know who you are, what you have, and what you want. And you must have the tools needed to attain those objectives. This is my simplistic definition of maturity. A given level of physical and mental stability is required to stay on the road toward reaching your set of goals. There are so many pitfalls and landmines that you cannot persevere if you let things pull you down or distract you. Maturity allows you to be content with what you have, while you work to improve your condition. There is no time to be jealous or envious of others. The mature person who succeeds is willing to help others find their way as well. Mature people do not brag or hold grudges. Maturity prevents you from pretending to be what you are not. It does not look for excuses to explain your shortcomings. Maturity gives you strength of character to overcome difficulties and remain focused on the given set of goals, no matter what may be in store for you.

Forgiveness

No matter how careful, well-intentioned, or well-mannered you are, you are bound to make mistakes and offend others. And people will offend you as well. The wise and sensible approach is to forgive and forget. In order to enjoy life, it is good to be humble enough to recognize your shortcomings, ask for forgiveness, repair the damage if that's possible, and move on. People who hold grudges constantly ruminate over what others are doing or did to them. These people wind up miserable, angry, and bitter. This type of thinking may even affect your health and psyche. Families, especially, are often poisoned by harboring resentments. Life is already too bumpy, complicated, and short to be run by bitterness. Forgiveness is like a glass of fresh water after a long walk on a hot and humid day. Forgiveness contributes to your success, because you feel free to seek help from anyone and to help anyone in need. It is not easy to forgive and forget; nevertheless, it is worth trying.

Friendship

John Donne wrote, "No man is an island." It is interesting that human beings continue to interact with each other in such a technologically advanced age. You need a few friends who can share your success and cheer you up in times of defeat and sorrow. The ideal friend is discrete, understanding, and loyal. Unfortunately, not many people have the necessary attributes to be reliable friends. A friend can save you, and a friend also can bury you. Here is a set of criteria to help you in the search for a good friend:

1. You know yourself and your limits, as well as what you can and cannot offer someone, and what you expect from others.

2. You recognize authentic friendship. The authentic friend is always looking out for you and your well-being, is honest and courageous, and enjoys your company. A friend accepts you just the way you are and vice versa.

3. You and a friend share common interests, goals, and dreams.

4. You know how to listen, forgive, forget, and not be self-serving; and so does your friend.

5. You and a friend understand that natural differences in character exist; you are able to allow time for adjustments and to respect each other's opinions, without resorting to personal attacks.

6. You both acknowledge that friendship is not a one-way street.

7. You both allow room for individual growth. True friendship encourages and stimulates personal growth. True friends share emotions, worries, successes, and failures.

8. You realize that even though friendship does make you vulnerable, some secrets and personal issues can never be shared with another human being.

Discipline

Success is accessible; wisdom is a precious gift. Neither one, however, comes to you on a silver platter.

Acquiring these attributes takes years of perseverance and experience. You must take some specific steps to make it in life. We can imagine the best projects in life, design the best blueprints, and spend our entire lives talking about them. Nothing will happen, though, without action. The key to result-oriented action is discipline. Discipline includes a set of self-imposed principles, rules of conduct, and values that allow you to follow a given pathway to reach your goals. This is the skeletal structure of success. It requires consistency and perseverance in good times as well as in bad. As a disciplined person, you are absorbed by a sense of urgency to fulfill your obligations. You know that the world is governed by some key principles. No one can succeed while neglecting responsibilities. You need to identify them and perform them, while avoiding any abuse of your privileges.

Action

Action is the placenta that gives birth to success. It stimulates you to labor. It pushes you to seek and choose the best strategies, establish priorities, remain realistic, meet challenges head on, and accept various sacrifices to meet the objectives. The world is full of people who talk about their great ideas day in and out but never take action. You cannot leave your success at the mercy of luck. Every successful step will help you to move forward. There is no time to let down your guard and become complacent and arrogant.

Spirituality

You already know that your mental and psychological condition affect your physical state. The power of mind over matter is well established. As human beings, we are vulnerable. You are powerless against time and the unforeseen events of life. Physical, emotional, and financial challenges can come upon you out of nowhere. When this happens, you cannot take refuge in denial. Even if you have perseverance, patience, maturity, flexibility, a positive attitude, and motivation, experience will tell you that sometimes, despite all the best attributes, you still feel empty, depressed, drained, and subdued. The missing ingredient, that little extra to give flavor and color to your life, is an inner need to be able to call upon a supernatural power. In his book *The God Gene: How Faith Is Hardwired Into Our Genes*, behavioral geneticist Dean H. Hamer states that spirituality is built into man's genetic code. Hamer believes that we have an innate capacity for spirituality. The fight for success contains many surprises and has many unpredictable twists and turns; a supernatural force can help you resist and stay the course until the end. Many people are thought to be successful, yet because of an unfilled void, turn to suicide. You need an anchor that is based on your beliefs, your culture, your values, your ethics, and your relations. You and you alone must develop your level of faith in the almighty Creator or a supernatural force, who can sustain you through the tremendous trials and tribulations of life.

Gratitude

Today's popular culture revolves around sensationalism and individual prowess. In that rush towards individual achievement and recognition, the majority of those who make it forget their humble beginnings. They often forget those who helped them on their way up. If you forget where you came from, if you neglect those who were there for you when things were tough and slow, then your success is valueless. No one can make it up there without the help of others. There are parents, friends, advisers, coaches, and even books that help. You need to be grateful and gracious to all of those who helped you. Arrogance, selfishness, and pride only lead to destruction. Gratitude is the glue that keeps you connected to others. It is the bridge that keeps us connected with those who were there for us in the past and who are likely to be there in the end. After all, fame, riches, and power are like vapor. Relationships and the way you treat others determine your real success.

Authenticity

Someone who is pressed from many corners and pulled in various directions tends to be an actor, playing different roles and singing different tunes, depending on the setting and the environment. Don't do that. You must consciously choose to be yourself. When the curtain closes and the excitement is over, you need to be able to look at yourself in the mirror and be at peace with yourself. Do not bluff and manipulate. You must, of course, know how to speak to people, how to treat others, be candid, and remain humble. It will not be easy, but keep trying. Many people prefer to listen to lies, to the spin, to what is politically correct. This is the easy path. You should resist the easy way and be true to yourself, even when you may be deemed stiff and boring. It may take longer for you to reach your dreams than others, but you must remember to be true to yourself. Those who know the authentic diamond will not settle for a fake.

Manners

In this world of moral pluralism and alternative lifestyles, where everything is being questioned, conventional behavior seems to have become unconventional. The line between acceptable and unacceptable behavior has blurred. How often are you watching TV or attending a game or a show when suddenly you become appalled by the conduct of your favorite star? People wonder about the demise of manners in today's world. The current trend seems to reward rudeness, selfishness, inconsiderateness, and discourtesy. Bad influences have become the norm. Many, especially younger people, do not seem to be aware of the existence of a better choice. Even those who are taught good manners at home seem to leave them behind their door before they go out.

It does not have to be this way. The world has enough of this type of behavior. You should choose to be different. Your presence should be a breath of fresh air in a polluted, intoxicated environment of ill-mannered people. Decency and civility are not signs of weakness. The way you dress, talk, and walk; your body language; your vocabulary; and the tone of your voice all project a loud message that you cannot convey otherwise. Please remember that it is always good to be nice. Make the world a better place through your manners.

Impediments to Human Success

Here are seven most common ways people mess up their lives:

1. Poor self image, emotional incontinence and instability: character.

2. Intolerance to criticism and ignoring their weaknesses.

3. Self indulgence, complaisance.

4. Lack of preparation.

5. A false sense of invulnerability.

6. Failure to self govern, manage one's power and privileges.

7. Failure to reconcile with their past and deal with unresolved issues.

Regardless of your intentions, a number of patterns can lead to a disastrous life.

Self

The main impediment to success often boils down to yourself. Please hear me out. We are often our own worst enemy. Everyone chooses a way according to personal choices. But choices have consequences, and everyone must also pay the price for those choices. Certain actions or inactions take you toward hell. It is easier to destroy your reputation than it is to build up. Personal character flaws can be the dynamite that blows away in a few seconds what took you years to build. How many times have you met charming people, geniuses with great ideas, talent, and skill, yet they are in a deplorable condition? Why? Because of cherished bad habits, lack of self-control, unfortunate personality and temperament. Have you seen extraordinary men reach the pinnacle of their accomplishment, yet because of misconduct and a moment of weakness, the rug is pulled from under them and everything tumbles down like a house of cards? Pride, revenge, jealousy, selfishness, covetousness, neglect, fear, doubt, and a lack of respect for others and for established norms will prevent you from making it.

To be successful, you need to be prepared and have the frame of mind of a successful person. You need to be objective and know yourself. You must take into account your health, your education, and your financial standing. You must surround yourself with people who have positive values and who are brave enough to tell you not what you want to hear but the naked truth. And you must be willing and able to take it as it comes.

Debt

The current trend is to buy now and pay later. Faced with sophisticated advertising and marketing techniques, many people succumb to the impulse and buy. People discover urges they didn't even know they had and they act on them. They wind up buying superfluous items and acquiring huge debt. There is a difference between what is necessary to live and the unlimited desires in life. Our desires are not determined by our means to pay.

Many lives have been ruined through debt. People have been enslaved by the various credit cards and plans aimed at attracting them to live way beyond their means. If you owe on many credit cards, it is time to take steps toward eliminating them.

1. Freeze all purchases.

2. Compare the interest rates and fees among your accounts and transferring those with higher rates to those with much lower rates. Then take a pair of scissors and destroy the cards with higher rates so you won't ever be tempted to use them.

3. Start paying more than the bare minimum required. This reduces the monthly surcharges and shortens the length of the debt.

4. Control your impulses. No more improvised shopping. No more impulse purchases.
   Plan ahead, make a written list of the items

you need to purchase. When you purchase an item on the list, write down where you purchased it and what you paid.

5. Do not leave your home with extra cash to go window shopping. Stick to your original list and watch out with who you are hanging out with; beware of friends who are overspenders and believe they deserve the treats.

6. Adopt direct deposit of your salary when possible, and limit your withdrawals to what is absolutely necessary.

7. Take steps to reduce the nonessential monthly expenses such as extra trips, eating out, the cinema, cell phones, and cable. (For example, if you can cut down on your late night TV time, you may get to sleep earlier and wake up early enough to prepare lunch and breakfast at home, instead of spending so much money eating out.)

8. Don't be profligate with your charity, especially when mortgaging your future. Your help should go primarily to those who take steps to help themselves and are willing to let you have an idea of their financial lifestyle and activities.

9. Consolidate your debts when it is clear that doing so will save you money by lowering your overall interest rate.

10. Act responsibly and resist the fallacy that you work too hard and you need to indulge yourself by engaging in activities and transactions that only mortgage your future.

Gambling

When going through financial hardships, there is a tendency to act desperately by throwing everything you have left onto one desperate bet—whether it's the sucker bet of the weekly lottery or the sure thing of a business proposition in an industry you don't know anything about. Gambling away the little you have should not be an option. Gambling is only reliably profitable to those who promote and control the game. If you put the few dollars you have into a savings book, at least it will still be there when you look for it. That is not the case with gambling.

Lack of insurance

Being low on funds is reason to abandon common sense. No one knows the future. You may face illness, unemployment, disability, fire, acts of God, and even death. Do your best to face it. Having a decent insurance policy within your means that can help you face those difficult moments is a step in the right direction.

Lawsuits

Life is becoming more and more difficult. As needs increase, costs increase, while the revenues tend to head in the opposite direction. Accidents happen at no one's fault or because of recklessness. Nevertheless, people have ways to seek compensation. Put aside technicalities, guilt, irresponsibility, and false cases. People sue for monetary compensation. Umbrella insurance is advisable. Furthermore, there are chances that must never be taken. You should never ever drive a car without an insurance policy; nor should you have a house without fire insurance. All in all, you should at least follow your government guidelines and the law enforcement policies in the place you live.

Taxes

Make sure you pay your taxes. There are legal ways to reduce the amount. Seek the help of an expert; but do not engage in any activities that can get you in trouble with taxing authorities. Tax avoidance is allowed, but tax evasion is a crime.

Credit profile

Although the general rule is to avoid debt as much as possible, there are transactions that require contracting debt. One of the ways to get the best deal and the best loan at the lowest rate is to have a good credit score. The credit score is derived from your credit profile. This is a record, maintained by national credit bureaus, of your standing with companies that have extended you credit, mostly banks and credit card companies. If you never borrow money or purchase anything on credit, you will not have a credit profile. If you do not have a credit profile, you will not be able to borrow money for major purchases. So it is important to build a credit profile by making small, affordable purchases on credit. As long as you pay what you agree to pay your creditors on time every month, your credit score continues to improve. Frequent instances of lateness affect your credit. How much do you owe and to whom? What is your debt ratio compared to your income? What is the ratio of your liabilities to your assets? Are you struggling to make the minimum payments by borrowing from one card to pay for another? Have you ever filed bankruptcy? How many obligations do you have? All of those factor into your overall credit score.

Basic advice for maintaining a good credit profile:

1. Make a credit purchase when you have the money ready to pay as soon as the bill comes.

2. Never pay your bills late, especially your mortgage.

3. Never contract debt or use your information to guarantee a loan for somebody else. You become as liable as the other party who asks you to cosign.

4. Do not take any financial discrepancy lightly. Reconcile and clear all questionable transactions.

5. Be careful about how you dispose of or display your personal information and to whom.

6. Keep your receipts and documents in a safe and specific place where you can find them when needed.

Your Personal and Financial Success

No normal human being will jump into an ocean and then discover he cannot swim. Embarking on life requires some basic common sense. There must be an overall plan, a projection for ten, twenty, thirty years from the starting point. When we take a look at life in the leading western world country, ideally, individual life is summed up as follows:

- *Childhood*—Preparation for life, which includes belonging to a household, primary and secondary schooling, and college.

- *Young adulthood*—By the time you reach twenty-two, either you are going for advanced study or you settle down and get ready to start your own generation's lifestyle—holding on to a steady job, having a significant other, having children, buying a house—and life goes on. If you do not intend to go to graduate school for a master's degree and a doctorate, you must be diligent enough to identify a field, a profession, a career that suits you to engage in steadily.

- *Middle age*—By the time you reach your fifties or sixties, you can choose to look forward to retiring from that job because you have accumulated enough years to qualify for a package and go on with your life and do whatever else you want, while you still have all or most of your marbles.

So, it is advantageous and wise to know what you want early.

Regardless of the domain in life you want to consider, your financial situation will always play a key role. It is the basis for your way of life. How much money would you like to make at age thirty, forty, fifty, and beyond? How much do you want in savings? Where do you really want to live? How big a house, and how many bedrooms do you want in your primary villa? What kinds of music, furniture, and paintings do you like? Where would you want to have your secondary or tertiary residence? How often would you like to go on vacation or visit your favorite spots in the world? How big do you want your ranch to be? Where would you keep your private plane? What about your boat? What types of investments attract you? What causes would you support? How much would you like to contribute to your community?

These questions—and many more—may come to mind as you flirt with your dreams. Do you ever stop to analyze them deeply or do you just brush them off as nightmares or forbidden dreams? If you want to be successful in life, you must have very big dreams. If you want to reach your goals, a solid financial foundation must play a key role. This solid foundation starts with a desire to meet some basic emotional needs; this may be a thought that grows and grows to the point of pushing you to take action to reach your goals. Generally, this foundation grows one block at a time.

Daily, weekly, and monthly exigencies

- Current income versus current expenses.
- Current savings.
- Current investment.
- Current debts.
- How to face emergencies.
- Current net worth and projected wealth.

Not long ago, some of my friends and family members and I went to a boat show. As I was walking around, I overheard one of the children ask his dad the following: "Dad, why are we here? You know we will never have a boat. We can't even pay our rent."

The father, a bit embarrassed, just ignored him. But his face turned all red. He took a deep breath, then he replied, "We'll have one much sooner than you think!"

Way before you can physically palpate the object; it is worth the confidence of working toward it instead of panicking for lack of ways and means to get it.

Baseline goal: increase earnings while decreasing expenses going forward

Look at:

- Current net worth versus future worth in one to ten years.
- Becoming debt-free in a specific period of time.

The above considerations must not only address your current lifestyle, but they also must factor in your desired future lifestyle. Your present is the result of your past, as your future will be based on your present choices and actions. Because your current lifestyle is building your future, the present requires enough foresight to anticipate your desired lifestyle in two, five, or ten years. The appropriate grasp of your present financial context helps determine what you need to do to be financially secure. Clearly visualize your expectations in terms of wealth, if not in exact amount. Then you need to get going to fulfill those expectations.

How much money are you making now? What is your current equity? How much are your total monthly expenses? What is your net worth? How much money do you need to retire with your idea of a decent life? What should you invest in? What happens if a disaster occurs? How do you finance your children's education? To answer these questions advantageously and become financially secure, you need to do your homework and learn to be financially educated. Following are some basic facts.

The source of your money

There are only a few legal and decent ways to obtain money. You can receive it as a gift, win the lottery, find it somewhere, or win a lawsuit. For various reasons, few people fall into these categories. Almost everyone has to work hard to make money to meet their needs. The amount of money you make seems as if it is never enough to fulfill all your desires. Nevertheless, the goal is to make the most money possible in a satisfying job with a decent schedule and manage that money well.

To begin, what kind of work are you doing now? Are you self-employed? Are you an entrepreneur? Are you a professional? Are you working for others? At what level of your job's hierarchy are you functioning? Is there room for advancement or is it a dead end? What can you do to improve your condition and position? Time is always constraining. What is the most efficient way to optimize your income and broaden your satisfaction with the most efficient use of your time? Teenagers generally work for fun and to get some extra cash for mundane stuff. A few people may work because they are bored. More likely, you work because you need to put a roof over your head, some clothes on your body, some food in your stomach, and to provide for your family. In short, you work to satisfy your basic needs. But when facing endless desires and limitless wants, you often go beyond those basic needs. The world is geared toward self-satisfaction and instant gratification. When you are making just enough money to survive, you might engage in transactions that are beyond the limit of your purchasing power. As a result, the job with the minimal salary, minimal or no benefits, and no room for growth becomes a life-time position, instead of a temporary stepping-stone. When this happens, you have come to a point where even your basic needs have changed. Your obligations are so heavy that you are trapped in a situation with no end in sight.

A woman complained to me that her limited fixed income did not meet her expenses. When I asked her to present her expenses, she mentioned her cable bill, cell phone bill, and credit card bills. She said nothing about rent, clothes, and food.

Decide on your ideal job or career. You must know who you are and what kind of a lifestyle you want.

Note the type of environment you find acceptable. For instance, if you like to work by yourself without interference, you should think twice before becoming a customer service representative or a counselor. You must:

1. Identify the profession that you want to work in, while taking into consideration the fact that some types of work pay more than others. Some also require more hours, more commitment, and more education.

2. Take the necessary steps to be fully qualified in the field of your choice. Be realistic and do not disregard an entry-level position. If you are dedicated, you will work your way up to your desired position.

3. Look for a job through recommendations and advertisements. Make all of the necessary phone calls, emails, etc. You have to sell yourself for people to know you. It may take some time, but do your homework and keep at it. The rest will take care of itself.

4. Work on your grooming, hygiene, posture, and behavior, if you are called in for an interview. During the interview, be confident, not cocky. Be assertive but not argumentative.

Express knowledge of and interest in the company rather than starting out with "What's in it for me" questions about vacations, benefits, and salary.

An interview is a conversation between equals. The interviewer wants to find out about you, and you want to find out about the company and the job. It's an exchange of information, not an inquisition.

In any negotiation about money, the first person to name a number loses. So don't start by saying how much you want to earn. Start by asking the range that the position pays. Know the minimum that is acceptable to you. If you are not offered that minimum and cannot negotiate for it, walk away rather than accept a job for less than what you need to earn.

Remember that you are looking for a job that you like, where there is room for advancement and the possibility of a lifetime career. You cannot be desperate; it is better to hold on to your bread and butter job while taking your time to search for your ideal job. Remember that the ideal job allows you to do what you really like while making enough to face the other challenges in your life.

5. Be quick to learn the routine, once you find your dream job. Be eager to take appropriate advice; beware of lateness, long coffee breaks, sick days, and standing in front of the time clock to count the remaining minutes of your day. Remember that the factors of promotion include knowledge, behavior, personality, and the ability to work unsupervised. Keep romance, gossip, and mood swings away from the office. Do not be too concerned about following those who have been there longer than you, especially when it comes to their bad habits. Some of those people may be at a dead end, counting the days or the months until their retirement.

Finally, never forget that the first impression always counts. Especially if it is a good one, it will carry you far.

6. Be willing to help others. This is often your opportunity to learn the duties of others and score points with your employers. Be willing to work extra hours, especially in the beginning.

I remember the first time I met a specific clerk in the bank where I have my account. When the boss told her to take care of my transaction, she replied, "It's my lunchtime." She was unlikely to get a promotion with such an attitude. No boss wants to hear, "It's not my job," "I've done my share," or "I work here from nine to five; my overtime is for my home." Often, just a little extra touch or service once in a while accounts for an unexpected raise, bonus, or promotion.

You have done your work well. You have made a difference in your company. Based on the overall situation, you deserve a raise and you need to know how to go about it. Usually there is a six-month or one-year evaluation. If you are going to ask for a raise, do it a bit earlier than that formal review of your performance. If you already have a two-percent raise coming, based on your evaluation, changing it to ten percent or getting a promotion is not going to be easy.

You have a job and you are making money, but that is not enough. You need to work toward your ultimate goal. Do you want to be an executive? Do you want to be self-employed? How much money is a decent amount for you? What kind of salary are you after? Whatever you want, you need to start working toward it and behave accordingly from the beginning. There is a way to dress, speak, behave, and write if you want to be an executive. If you are always late, call in sick every month, clock out first, complain about the amount of work you do, spend a lot of time on the phone for personal matters, and dress like a homeless person, how can you expect the board of directors to promote you to chief executive or chief financial officer? And if they don't, you can't call it discrimination, either! No one wants to run the risk of bringing down a company because he chooses the wrong person to promote. Those kinds of positions require knowledge, loyalty, and resourcefulness, the ability to face challenges, emotional stability, communication skills, and empathy.

Other sources of money for the mature you

When it comes to money, the ideal situation is to make as much as possible, to the point that it works for you even in your sleep. You may not live long enough to see that day. But there are other ways to administer money to your advantage. As you navigate your way through the financial world, realize that your worth is based on your income and your equity versus what you owe. Wait a minute! No need to be confused. I said before that you must stay away from debt. That was a bit of a simplification to help you develop solid financial habits that will help you grow. However, on your way toward a better financial standing, some acquisitions—a house, for example, or a business—are too large for an ordinary person to pay cash. They require a partial payment with the obligation to pay the difference though a number of months or even years. History shows us countless examples of people who were able to jump on a great opportunity because of the availability of a loan. To make such a loan, lenders need your credit profile.

Another source of money: other people's money

"Money isn't everything!" When I hear that, I say, "Try me, I'll show you!" If you are physically and mentally healthy, money is the best thing that can happen to you, providing you know what to do with it. Personal wealth is scarce; you try your best to make and to keep as much money as possible. But you are still going through a lifelong struggle, so you build a credit track record. You have goals. Sooner or later, you realize that inflation raises the cost of living, and the purchasing power of money keeps decreasing. Hard currencies cannot keep pace with those independent factors. You need to diversify. You need to invest. You need to move up the ladder. You cannot stay static.

You have made the money, how do you use it?

It is a common belief that if you make enough money you will be able to face all of your obligations. Those who believe such an idea are naïve, to say the least. In the twenty-first century, even basic human needs can be satisfied in either a simple or a fancy way. For example, the outfit for one person for one event may cover the cost of someone else's first home. Desires are unlimited. The more you have, the more you want to have. The secret is not necessarily in how much you make, but in what you do with what you earn. In the book of Matthew, chapter 20, Jesus talks about three kinds of servants. One has five talents, another one has three, and the last one has one talent. He goes on to say, "To those who have, more will be given. To those who have not, even the bare minimum they have will be taken away from them" Many are shocked to read such a sentence from the Holy Book. And to make things worse, those words came out of the mouth of Jesus, who is known for His words and work towards defending the poor. It takes a while to digest the idea. It stems from the basic principle that if you cannot manage the little you have, what makes you think you will be able to manage a lot more? Many lottery winners go back to their previous lifestyle because they are not ready to adjust to their new wealth.

It is not enough to make a lot of money; the key is how it is disbursed. If you mishandle a small amount, you are much more likely to mismanage a lot.

One common approach is to have a system whereby you allocate a percentage of your take-home pay to community service, a percentage to savings, and the rest for routine obligations. A well-known formula for this system is called "10-10-80." This means that you donate 10 percent, save 10 percent, and pay bills with 80 percent. You must then see to it that you run your life efficiently enough to live within the 80 percent. Using less than 80 percent to cover expenses means you can save and invest more, which is highly desirable.

You cannot live an isolated life while ignoring the society, community, and neighborhood in which you live. Many factors may determine your place of residency. In any given community, there is a symbiotic relationship between the members of such a community and the individuals who form it. The appearance of the community, its reputation, the average age of its occupants, its values, its primary religious denomination, and its youth orientation all contribute to the destiny of the neighborhood. Therefore, as a resident in a given milieu, you should contribute to its betterment. Your 10 percent contribution can help support ministerial activities, worthy causes based on your beliefs, and your personal interests.

Once you are working and receiving an income, or even if you are receiving an allowance, you must have a personal investment portfolio. Your financial independence and your economic success are based on your savings and your investments. Do not wait for millions; any little bit helps. The earlier you start, the better off you are. Did you know that if you consistently save one hundred dollars a month at age twenty, by the time you reach the retirement age, you are likely to have one million dollars in savings? But if you start at age thirty, you need six times that much; at forty, you need about four hundred dollars a week; at fifty, you need thirteen hundred dollars a week. And if you start earlier, you will of course make that money much sooner. These consistent savings will add up with interest compounded regularly. Remember, the expenses of the young often deal with appearances, depreciable goods, and services; you can generally do without these expensive clothes, cars, apartments, and furniture.

A mother and father worked very hard to encourage their child to finish high school. They refinanced their house to send him to college so that he could go on to law school. During this time, they did not ask their son to take out a loan. The son is a very bright young man, who passed the bar exam on his first try. Shortly after he landed a good job at a prestigious firm, and to his parents' dismay, he immediately moved out of their house into one of the most expensive parts of town. He also bought a car and all the fine things in life. His lifestyle had apparently changed for the better, except for the fact that he lived from paycheck to paycheck, with no savings. Within a short time, he was deep in debt, and the parents were stuck with the refinancing adventures alone. This young man, of course, had alternatives to the way this situation played out; he could have taken a more practical and wise approach. He could have used public transportation instead of buying an expensive car, shopped at less expensive clothing stores, and cut down on eating out. Depending on his relationship with his parents, he could have even lived with them for awhile in order to save money.

But many people cannot resist the virus of instant gratification; they live by the theory that there is only one life to live and they should enjoy it now and worry about savings later. It does not have to be that way. You can enjoy life with savings. The enjoyment is more delightful when you can be part of the investors' club at a young age. It is a great feeling to be young, debt-free, and able to save on a regular basis and to have a respectable investment portfolio. Early in life you must be resolute in saving 10 percent of whatever you earn. If you can save a higher percentage of your income, it is even better. The more you save now, the greater the rewards will be later.

Not only must you save at least 10 percent of your earnings, but also you need to know how to make your savings earn the maximum profit. When you are old, you may not have a salary coming in, and the cost of living will definitely be higher. You will have unforeseen expenses and may have health issues, too. How many times do you hear about elderly people having to make a choice between food and medication? It should not be that way. No one should have to choose between eating properly and buying medication.

Consult an expert. Based upon your risk-taking ability, you may choose specific savings accounts, money market accounts, treasury bonds, certificates of deposit, stock options, and real estate. You should also include life insurance, personal liability insurance, health insurance, etc.

In addition to consulting a trustworthy specialist, you can learn a lot on the subject from the Internet or from books and magazines. Schools and parents often fail to teach the next generation about personal finances, particularly money management.

Human beings naturally have insatiable desires. The more you see, the more you see others have, and therefore the more you want. Your core limitation is simple. Your needs do not provide the means to acquire them. After your charitable donations and your savings, the remaining 80 percent of your income must be spent wisely. To give it more power, you need to compare prices and quality, ask, shop around, learn from others, know where to eat, and only buy what is needed. This is where the concept of budget comes into play. It means you must refrain from impulsive buying and frivolous spending without a plan.

The elements of a budget are simple. There is no need to shy away from it. Suppose—for the sake of argument—you earn a monthly income of $2,000 after taxes. Out of this sum, you donate $200 and you save $200. The key now is how to allocate the remaining $1,600. The main items you need include housing, utilities, food, transportation, childcare, healthcare, clothing, and other necessities. When money is tight, leisure activities, dining out, entertainment, and so forth, are the items to eliminate or reduce. With a limited budget, there is hardly any room for impulse buying. Don't feel bad about it, and don't let peer pressure get the best of you. Could you imagine, with such a tight budget, deciding to use credit cards left and right? As a normal, reasonable person, you should not voluntarily subject yourself to the slavery of chronic debt and the stress and anxiety that comes with it. Financial discipline is the only way to build up financial independence and prosperity.

Your other alternative is to get more money. When you work for someone else, you can do that by expanding your responsibilities, getting extra work, or getting a raise or a bonus. Even then, let your common sense get the best of you! By all means, consider each option thoroughly before making a move, without being a miser. You do not want to contribute to your own setbacks. You must often walk a thin line between making it big or going through setbacks. But no matter what, if you know where you want to go, you can always get back on track.

Real Estate Acquisition

Buying real estate can improve your status and build up your assets. Buying a house not only provides you with a place to live, but it also tends to appreciate in value with time and positively affect your income tax return too. Buying or selling a house is an exciting and challenging opportunity. Your choice of a home depends on:

1. **The cost, the financing, and your income bracket**— Because you are likely to seek a mortgage, the lending institution will take a careful look at your income, your work history, and your credit rating. Each institution has its own formula that it uses to determine whether or not you can afford the dwelling you chose. As far as you are concerned, you need to conduct your research and get satisfactory answers to some key issues: What kind of mortgage are you getting? What institution provides it, a private or government-backed facility? What is the cheapest available? What type of loan do you need—a fixed rate or variable rate? Is there a broker (middleman) involved? What are the declared fees and the hidden fees? Beware of those who want to sell to you and at the same time are referring you to a financial institution for the mortgage. Are there any incentives or discounts for you as a first-time buyer? What is the zoning

code? Are there restrictions regarding the required time to be an owner occupying the house? Etc.

2. **The given geographical area where you want to buy property**— One thing you are quickly going to discover upon deciding to buy a house is that the price ranges vary with the location. Depending on the state, community, and area, your cost will fluctuate and will somehow affect your choices. It is worth factoring in the time and whether it is a buyers' market (when the sellers want to sell as quickly as possible, based on some economic signs and personal constraints) or a sellers' market (when the seller wants to hold on and try to get as much as possible for a given property).

3. **Your individual tastes and plans**— You already have an idea of the type of house you want. You have your preferences; you want the bedrooms to be a certain size and a certain distance from the bathroom. Maybe you want a backyard, garage, driveway, and completely detached or semi-detached house. Maybe you prefer a big house with many bedrooms, many bathrooms, and walk-in closets. If you have children, you probably want to live not too far from a good school and in a decent neighborhood. If you have older children, you have other concerns. Based on your age and health condition, you may want to rent or live in a condominium or in a community-based setting. To have an idea of the neighborhood, try to pass by over the weekend or late at night, and see what is happening in the streets nearby. Take a look at how the neighborhood pets are treated, the treatment of the children, and the behavior

of the young people in the neighborhood. All in all, our unique tastes will express themselves in our acquisition. The first acquisition may not fit all your criteria. Be very careful; buying a home is not like buying a toaster or a television set. Make sure the roof, plumbing, heating and cooling system, and the wiring are all in excellent condition. Hire an expert to check and inspect everything. When in doubt, have your attorney hold some money in escrow for a few weeks or months until everything is clear. Do not accept any oral promises. Keep your eye on the ultimate goal: building up a secure financial estate for you and possibly the next generation. When you are buying a home, you need to keep some things in mind:

- You have to have a lump sum to give as a down payment, often as much as ten percent of the total price.

- You have to pay a variety of fees both before and during the closing, including attorney's fees, appraisal fees, title search fees, etc. Ask about these ahead of time so you know how much money you have to have available to cover them.

- You need to allow for real estate taxes, homeowners' insurance, utilities, repairs, maintenance, and emergencies. Add up all of these in determining your ability to buy the home.

- You have to allow for the cost of moving into the newly acquired house.

- The monthly mortgage is usually due the first of every month, starting one to two months after closing.

Your best approach is to sit down and figure out most of the expenses. You are better off overestimating rather than underestimating your expenses. Resist the urge to invite friends over to celebrate and put yourself under pressure to have the house completely furnished for the event; by doing this you may put yourself in debt. Remember, friends come, friends look and talk, but friends do not want to hear about your financial troubles. When you move in, if you have to sleep on the floor until you can bounce back and start to recuperate financially, do it. You just made a great investment. You should be proud of yourself. It is another step in the right direction. Be ready to enjoy it. But when the time comes, also be ready to sell it later on for various reasons, provided the price is right. Such a transaction will contribute toward reaching your ultimate goal.

Refinancing

There is a lot of advertising out there that offers refinancing services for homeowners. These offers often sound attractive, and many homeowners decide to go for it. Refinancing is a double-edged sword. On the one hand, if you owe credit and collections companies, you have various types of loans at different rates. If you are barely paying the minimum, it seems reasonable to consolidate all these bills by refinancing. But what happens after such a transaction? What guarantees do you have that you will not fall into the same rut a few years down the line with an increased liability on the only investment most of us have ever had? Or, what happens if the market value of your home drops for any reason? Carefully consider refinancing if:

- You owe enough to want to consolidate. You must find a way, either by being a strong-willed person and knowing how to stay away from the same path that got you there in the first place or by seeking counseling to avoid such failures in the future.

- You are not liquidating assets to meet current expenses. For example, you should not take money out on your house to go on a vacation, to buy a car, etc.

Refinancing is acceptable for either of two reasons:

- To get a better deal at a lower rate, after factoring in all of the clauses and hidden costs. Make sure it is worth it in the long run.

- To finance causes, such as career-related education, to increase your income potential and your overall assets.

Children's tuition may be considered under specific conditions. If they can get a loan at a zero-percent rate, with no hidden fees and no penalty if paying upon graduation, let them get the loan. A few years from now, the value of your house is likely to increase, giving you more available equity, while you will pay then the exact amount of money you get now.

As a general rule, anytime you can get a lump sum of money now to pay back that same amount with no interest and no hidden fees a few years later, you should take it and put it in a savings account. When you pay it back, whatever interest it has made in the process is yours.

Finally, based upon the type of person you are and your ability to be involved in repeated transactions, that first house should be a starting point into acquiring various others. How can these happen? It will happen if you initially focus on investing and making money, instead of walking into a dream home once and for all. The business-minded individual, the go-getter, upon buying a house, sees in it a source of income. Based on how much you can put down, and taking into consideration what the combined established institutions (private and public) can offer, you may go for a two-family home or even a multiple dwelling. You can learn to live in the basement of a two-family house for a while, where that is permitted by local laws, and rent the two apartments at their market value while they appreciate. Continue to save as in the past. Your savings, added to the positive balance from the tenants and the tax breaks given to homeowners, plus the appreciation of the two-family home, can all add up to enough money for a down payment on another house some time later. But you must be willing to delay gratification. You must know what you are doing and you must not hesitate to seek available help when needed. Also do not make the mistake of accumulating cash and postponing the real estate acquisition, while the cost of buying a house keeps going up at a rate faster than your savings. Once you get enough money to buy a house, after doing your homework, and with the proper advice and guidance, buy it. Sometimes you may not even be able to buy in the neighborhood of your dreams. Take the first step. Housing often goes through a cycle. Just make sure you do the proper homework and get the right advice.

If you are selling, remember that some minor repairs, such as a new carpet and some painting, can automatically add hundreds—if not thousands—of dollars' value to the property. So do not be cheap and sloppy.

Buying a car

As you move up the ladder, you may decide to buy a car. Assuming you know how to drive and you have a license, why do you want to buy a car? This requires even greater scrutiny than buying a house, because the moment you drive a new car out of the showroom, it begins to lose value rapidly.

My wife and I went to buy a so-called luxury car a few years ago. The salesman coerced us into buying that specific car and we bought it. On our way home, my wife discovered that she did not like it because it was "too powerful, too sporty," and my head touched the ceiling each time the car ran over a pothole. Once we got home, we called the guy who sold it to us. He told us to bring it in whenever we had a chance. Because of our busy schedules, we took it back a few days later, and the car had depreciated by over four thousand dollars. This was the most expensive ride of our lives.

Even if you are really rich and your money works for you every second of the day, you must be careful in any transactions, including when you decide to buy a vehicle. Do you really need this car? What kind of car do you want? Do you know enough about that specific model? Have you figured out how much it will cost? What is the cost for full insurance in your neighborhood? How much money does the car cost in gas and repairs per month? Where are you going to park it? What are the features, including antitheft devices? Have you compared the cost of public transportation, car-pooling, and leasing options versus buying? Is there any reason to even consider acquiring a used car, and under what specific conditions? Why not lease? Even after you have answered all these questions to your satisfaction, go for a test drive. You must know where and when to buy in order to get the best deal; usually the current model, bought when the showroom must be emptied for the new models, is more affordable, although it also has a lower book value at the end of the model year. Also, you are likely to get a very good deal if you can write a check for the full purchase price (for example, if you arrange a bank loan before you buy the car). Some dealers prefer to sell cars with a zero- or low-down payment. The key is to go through the whole negotiation process until a final price is reached and then you make your full payment or talk about trading to avoid all those finance charges. Concerning trading in your current vehicle for a new one, do your homework. You may get more money if you sell your old model on your own than to exchange it at the dealer, for the obvious reason that the dealer wants it at the lowest cost possible so he can make a profit when he sells it.

How To Cement Long-Term Financial Success

You have chosen your career, you are saving systematically, you are helping the community, you are controlling your expenses, and you have real estate assets. Things look good. But there is always a "but." Yes, you have heard it before: "don't put all your eggs in one basket". After the Indonesian tsunami, 9/11, and other well-known regrettable events, you should be convinced not only that life is precious and fragile, but also that it does not take much to become homeless, uprooted, poor, and dispossessed. As if that were not bad enough, companies go belly-up and pensions are wiped out. Even social security is not a panacea. In the meantime, life expectancy increases, along with the cost of living. You need a broader, more practical and feasible plan to survive. What can you do for a decent tomorrow?

Remember the basics that we all share

1. Abraham Maslow postulated five sets of basic human needs: physiological needs, safety, love and belonging, esteem, and self-actualization.

2. Bad choices can torpedo your future. Avoid drugs, gambling, bad company, and risky behavior.

3. At some level, we all share the desire to last forever.

To make the right decisions, you need to take inventory of your current situation, clearly define your objectives, come up with a plan of action, and pursue it, while making the necessary adjustments. Financial success also requires the ability to avoid catastrophic turns that may lead to sudden death. Knowledge is power. Among the basic instructions, remember the following:

1. There is a difference between a simple savings book, with a reduced rate while your money remains theoretically available upon request, and properly investing your money at a much higher rate for a longer time. Bear in mind, the higher the reward, the higher is the risk.

2. There are rules to navigate on the agitated sea of investment. The smart investor:

    *   Knows himself and knows his ability to tolerate a possible bad outcome. He must calculate his risks.

    *   Begins as early as possible. If unsure, start small and slow. No wise person would drive a car before knowing how to drive.

    *   Educates and prepares himself and develops the appropriate plan. Visit the libraries, go online, and seek the assistance of an expert.

- Avoids pyramid schemes. Stays away from transactions that can bring him to the top overnight at the expense of others. Generally speaking, there is no such thing as spontaneous wealth.

- Resists the tendency to panic or to go berserk because of rumors. Knows what he knows and does what he knows. Does not rely on dreams or fads to make significant choices.

- Knows when to change horses. There should be no sentimental or emotional attachment to a given investment.

- Avoids addiction. He does not have to play the market all the time to the point of risking all he has and then borrow to continue losing.

- Risks only what he can afford to lose.

- Is prudent enough not to put all that he has in one investment.

In summary, to navigate safely in life, you need to aim high and shoot for the best, while preparing for the worst scenario. To do so, remember:

1. Learn to enjoy every available present moment; it is the elixir to make life enjoyable for all of those who come into contact with you. This will help you physically and emotionally and will contribute to your living to see that tomorrow.

2. Have a set of long-term financial goals based on the type of life you want.

By the time Joe and Jane retire, they will have paid off their house. Their expected monthly living expenses after retirement, for food, recreational activities, vacations, and health care, will amount to $2,000 a month. If *they expect a $500 check from social security, they must be able to come up with $1,500 on their own. How can they do that if they plan on leaving their house for their grandchildren? They must consider several alternative plans, taking into account their current age, the amount of their savings, their health, and other factors:*

- *Savings accounts that have interest compounded daily, so they have ready cash, easily accessible in case of a medical emergency.*

- *A well-balanced portfolio from a reputable financial institution.*

- *Health insurance.*

- *Life insurance.*

- *Disability insurance.*

- *Individual retirement accounts.*

- *Tax shelters.*

- *Funeral financing.*

Life is a journey with various sights to see. The ride can be smooth or bumpy. The key is to make ample provisions for the unknown, especially future financial condition. The wise thing to do is to take control of your financial situation now.

Love and Success

The Adolescent and Love

In this global society, a human's life is valued through the prisms of love, relationships, success, and legacy. But love, success, and legacy are truly appreciated through the lens of relationships. Your success, your love, and your legacy are based on the quality of your relationships.

No one wants to be alone. The types of relationships you maintain determine your level of fulfillment in life. By relationship, I mean the ability to have contact and dialogue with others. There are many different types as well as various levels of relationships. But for the sake of simplicity, we can classify your relationships with the people you encounter in day-to-day life into three categories—negative, neutral, and positive.

Negative relationships will drain you, put you down, give you an inferiority complex, and get you upset. They can make you sick and even cause your death if you are not careful.

Neutral relationships are those where you neither lose nor gain anything.

Positive relationships exert a dynamic influence on you. They make you want to reach the top of the tallest mountain, if not the moon. Of course, there will be some bad days and some bumps in the road. But when you consider all the issues at stake, there is no doubt that both parties come out as winners.

All of us obviously dream of the perfect relationship. In reality, it does not happen often because of many factors including: character, personality, culture, values, beliefs, genes, etc. Nevertheless, the more you invest in a relationship, the more vulnerable you become. The key is the type of relationship. This is where love comes in. Love sustains a relationship.

The concept of love

Falling in love is one of the inexorable laws of nature. You can talk about it, write about it, read about it; you can be against it, in favor of it, or well prepared for it. It does not matter. Sooner or later it will hit you and it will knock your socks off. So beware! It is an equal opportunity emotion that boils within each of us. It is there. It is not about the crush you had as a kid on your grade school teacher, your music professor, your coach, or your Sunday school teacher. Although some of those crushes can really take your feet off the ground for a while, the truth of the matter is that sometime around your adolescence, while you are being pulled in various directions by different forces, when you have so many unanswered questions, it suddenly hits you and knocks you out. With the advent of so many suggestive, sensual objects, there is even a tendency for love to hit you prematurely and find you unprepared.

When does it begin? No one knows exactly. You can only experience it when it happens.

It is a typical, sunny Sunday afternoon in the summer. Friends are getting together to go to the park to enjoy themselves and there are countless people at the beach— playing, dancing, sunbathing, swimming, eating, reading, or thinking. Ryan is having fun with his friends. Suddenly, out of nowhere, an angel appears and strikes his heart. She is wearing a dark blue T-shirt with the inscription "Fed up with men!" on the back, over a beige skirt that is quite a few inches above her knees. She has hazel eyes, perky lip, and a million dollar smile that exudes confidence and defiance. She is charming and beautiful. Ryan cannot figure out if he is in the clouds or on earth, if he is dreaming or awake. He feels simultaneously hot and cold. His heart is popping out of his chest. The sun becomes brighter. The flowers are more beautiful when they give off their sweet perfume. He can hear the birds' symphony. He feels as if a switch that he did not know existed just turned on inside of him, and everything is painted in bright and lovely colors. He is ready to engage in the pursuit of that angel. He is happy just at the appearance of that perfect creature. The two do not initially exchange many words. He is so dumbfounded that it takes him a while to remember his own name and gather the strength to introduce himself. After he meets Lisa, he forgets about his friends who are with him. He goes home and composes an email to her. To him, this is the best night of his life, with many more to come. He can only think about one person— the one who changed his life. He cannot fully describe or understand the way he feels. The hormonal awakening, the rush of such intense emotions, that magnetic pull toward Lisa is almost too great for him to bear. No words can translate his true feelings. The great emotions nearly choke him. Because of the constraints of unforeseen circumstances, Ryan can hardly wait for the following Friday evening to meet with her, take a much closer look at her, enjoy her smile and look into her eyes. He wants to know all about her, her friends, her parents, her hobbies, her family, what she likes, and best of all, whether or not there is some competition. Ryan quickly realizes he can no longer live without her. He has to call her, text message her, and email her almost constantly.

Lisa brings him happiness and energizes him. This Sunday afternoon encounter is the best gift Ryan has ever received, and he becomes happier and happier as time passes.

Finding your one true love is a fantasy that nearly everyone has either experienced or dreamed about. Books, magazines, movies, and television are full of tales about Prince Charming meeting Sleeping Beauty and the two of them loving each other and living happily ever after. In real life, things more often than not occur differently. When two hearts beat as one, it is an extraordinary gift that brings elation and hope to all. Real love, however, is not like the romantic songs that we hear constantly on the radio or from our MP3 players. True love requires certain conditions to blossom. Certain work must be done.

Time is a key factor in any lasting relationship. You need time to know yourself, to know your partner and your partner's strengths, shortcomings, habits, beliefs, skills, and talents. The initial emotional explosion that generates enough energy to light up an entire city is unfortunately not going to last forever. Love needs to be nurtured and well-maintained. It is easier to fall in love with a young, attractive person than to maintain a lasting relationship through emotional storms and the multiple challenges of daily life. Yesterday, everything was centered on the self, parents, friends, studies, toys, and play. But once Love walks in, things never stay the same. From then on, love presents constant challenges, and you must live up to those challenges. You must quickly adopt a mature approach to life. You discover that men and women are equal in rights and capacities, but different in a few ways other than their anatomical appearance. Their emotional and sentimental needs differ. A man, for instance, is naturally attracted by what he can see: voluptuous lips, breast size, physical shape and appearance, the walk, the smile, and the eyes. A woman, on the other hand, won't mind a handsome man, but she usually sees a man in a complete scenario: character, ability to love, protect, provide, understand, communicate, etc. Again, such differences do not make one sex inferior to the other. A person with a bigger body will proportionately have a bigger head and brain, but that does not confer superior intelligence or qualifications to one at the expense of the other.

When those two hearts meet and start dancing in unison to the rhythm of love, there are other desires that pop up as well. The strong desire to be with that person forever can also cause a lot of hurt and suffering. You probably remember some foolish instance of adolescent jealousy stemming from your own insecurity and the fear of losing your first love to another. Your strong love made you ready to fight and protect your territory.

The love that offers a lot also requires a lot. Unfortunately, many people tend to focus on what love offers rather than what it requires. Love needs time, yet it transcends time. Love must give, yet as individuals we want to receive. Our culture's tendency to always look out for number one makes it unlikely for love to reach its utmost level of beauty. Nowadays, boys meet girls casually, and there is little interest in lasting relationships. For many, sex is just a daily physiological need.

But true love is unique, and there is no magic formula. When adolescents meet their first serious love and its challenges, there needs to be a certain set of structured rules and guidance to protect them from serious shock. When we are young, we are usually full of life, energy, and adventure; we see life through rose-colored glasses. When you meet a new friend, what a joy! You are ready to go through every challenge. You have goals, dreams, desires, joys, and passions to share. Unfortunately, the ultimate outcome is not always happy. Although it is culturally accepted and promoted that in our youth we should have fun, meet new people, and acquire as many experiences as possible, the truth is that there is no free ride in life. You are responsible for your acts and you must account for them. You cannot play with love as you would with a baby doll or a spinning top. An unfortunate experience early in life may leave psychological (more rarely, physical) scars that affect your future life. It is paramount to know what to do to avoid pitfalls and to know what is necessary for a lasting love life.

We may face many stumbling blocks before we can obtain a gratifying love life. When we are young, many of us have the illusion that we are mature enough to make lasting and carefully discerned choices. As time passes, we tend to change ideals, tastes, and convictions. Once you fall in love, you must be mature enough to give your partner breathing room to grow during the relationship. True love facilitates intellectual progress, as well as emotional and physical maturity. Based on your character, goals, values, beliefs, and what you expect to find in a partner, you will discover many surprises. It is important to be willing to learn about each other, to communicate and share past habits, beliefs, apprehensions, wishes and expectations for a common future. A period of adaptation allows the couple to determine whether or not they are fit for each other. The latter also depends greatly on your initial intention. You must determine whether you are after a brief affair or a serious connection. Let this be known in the beginning, and you will avoid much hurt, bitterness, and scarring.

The twenty-first century has seen various kinds of love flourish in order to cope with the surprises of people living together.

Engagement

The notion of engagement goes back to the time of old family traditions. Throughout the ages, the engagement ceremony has seen some changes and modifications according to different cultures, customs, and civilizations. In the contemporary world, the engagement ceremony announces serious steps towards tying the knot. It represents a period of preparation for the big date. The young lady usually receives a beautiful engagement ring during this special moment. Some cultures bring family and friends together for a public proposal, in which the young man gets down on his knee to ask the big question, "Will you marry me?"

Men have found many exotic ways to propose—on the back of a city bus, in a helicopter, in a hot air balloon, on a radio or television program, with a skywriting message or a tattoo. Regardless of the medium, the sweethearts are on the verge of walking down the aisle to declare officially and publicly their commitment to live for each other until death separates them. During the engagement, the couple has to address certain pertinent questions, such as physical attraction, sharing of emotions, money management, ways of communicating, and conflict resolution. One key issue that still plays an important role in most relationships is sex.

When two normal people love each other, there is a natural physical attraction that causes them to want to be intimate with each other and surrender to one another without restriction. At this time the main question is, "When can you share everything—give it all and take it all?" This question still arises in certain relationships. It may be taboo for some, but for completeness, I'll address it. Right at the entry of the vagina—the female organ—there is a membrane called a hymen. It gives the seal of virginity to every young lady who has not been penetrated by a man's penis.

In the modern era, few people talk about this issue, and many doubt that chastity can even exist in this current, permissive world. A woman's virginity betokens a moral code; it makes a special statement that she has decided to remain chaste and to give herself truly to her special partner at a special moment. It is worth mentioning that there is a distinction between a mere physical virginity and a moral and psychologically authentic virginity. Although a woman may not have been physically penetrated, she can still be morally bankrupt. Authentic virginity is from the heart and spirit as well as from the body. Too often, this facet of life is neglected. Premature and inappropriate sexual relations can leave scars. And because success requires hard work, it is worth avoiding anything that can make it more difficult and require extra energy to overcome. This issue has to be addressed by each individual couple, based on the beliefs of the people involved, their moral values, and their culture, without any type of pressure.

During the engagement period, if the couple discover they are incompatible, they should put a stop to the whole thing instead of spending a lot of money on a wedding. You should get married for all the good reasons: love; companionship; shared aspirations, beliefs, and respect. Each person should get married in order to make their partner happy to the best of their ability. If your heart is not in it, you should avoid getting married. Don't marry because of unplanned pregnancy, or economic and familial freedom. If your partner behaves in a way that displeases you before marriage, your displeasure will likely grow after. Assuming that everything will fall into place after the wedding day is just wishful thinking. Marriage is a choice, and such a choice requires maturity, freedom, and lucidity.

Married life

Finally the moment has come; on a beautiful day two people choose of their own free will to join their lives together "for better or for worse." Such a picture never ceases to impress humanity. Family life always has had an impact on this planet.

No matter how we expand the definition of family, the family unit remains a viable entity. Changes in values have their consequences on the society as a whole. That the world contains so many delinquents, that so many jails are filled with prisoners, that there is crime and depravity in the current world can all be traced to a decline in family values. The divorce rate is high; many children grow up in a household with only one or no biological parent. Even in many two-parent households, the parents are always fighting, threatening each other, and making the environment stressful for the kids. In a society where home life is well balanced, legislation is appropriate, schools are well administered, the communities are well established, and moral values are paramount, we should expect better outcomes.

Generally, home is a place where a family lives. The concept of marriage has gone through some alterations and adjustments; nevertheless, it remains a viable institution, and this is why people still tie the knot. Look at those couples as they walk down the aisle to exchange their wedding vows. Usually they look happy; they are smiling, pretty, and convinced that they are on their way to happiness. Unfortunately, many of these marriages end up a complete failure. It is common sense to ask why. Why is there so much suffering, bitterness, unfaithfulness, and disappointment? Why are there so many divorces among those who just yesterday were so much in love, so inseparable, and so happy? Is the ideal home just a utopia? Can you ever avoid shattered dreams, broken hearts, frustration, and disgust?

Imagine three canoes floating on the sea; their goal is to go a given distance. On their way, they face obstacles—strong winds and currents. In each canoe sit two partners. In the first canoe, the partners are paddling opposite directions. In the second canoe, one partner is trying feverishly to get the canoe out of trouble while the other partner sits idly with his arms folded. And in the third canoe, the two partners forget about their differences, join together, and paddle in the same direction.

Which of these canoes is likely to get to its destination the safest and quickest? Obviously, the third one is likely to make it.

Let's take a quick look at the steps that lead to a wedding nowadays. People meet each other, they feel for each other, they get comfortable, and they want to get married. Sometimes they do not even bother to know about their partner's past, previous adventures, background, or family history. When these people meet, they pass their time in idle entertainment instead of getting to know each other. What is going to hold such a relationship together? The funny thing is, a significant number of people have an exit strategy before they even sign the marriage certificate; their lawyers are standing by with a prenuptial agreement. As long as you get married to please yourself, to get the most out of it, there will always be a time to get out of it for a better situation. When two people who grew up in two different households, with different genes, habits, and beliefs get together under one roof, there is no way things will magically become smooth and happy overnight. Most marriages end in less than ten years. It is a big obligation to get stuck with someone who all of a sudden must share your life. You have to suffer their shortcomings and bad habits; you have to help them in any instance. Only time becomes the best advisor. This is an era of speed. The effervescent tablet of divorce or separation is so readily available that often people don't stop for a moment to consider the alternative.

Four Key Steps Toward a Happy and Lasting Relationship

Know yourself and your baggage

After an unbiased assessment, with input from family members and close friends, closely analyze your character, habits, dreams, goals, purpose in life, opinion about yourself, level of maturity, personality, anger management, impulse control, weaknesses, and strengths; and then determine whether or not you are marriage material. Are you flexible, trustworthy, patient, altruistic, and conciliatory? Do you know how to show love, empathy, and appreciation? Do you know how to listen? Do you have core values, without being intransigent and self-righteous? Are you willing to learn, to improve on yourself, and to compromise? An affirmative response to these questions is a good start.

Identify what you want and expect in a relationship

Generally, people get into a conjugal relationship with a lot of hope. They smile and are looking forward to everlasting happiness. Yet this is far from the reality of the situation. It is necessary for you to know how committed you are, what you want from this relationship, and to communicate it to the other person. If two partners get involved with the determination to make their relationship work, it is a step in the right direction. Put into perspective the kind of home you expect, the responsibilities, the potential careers, the issue of children, what you like and do not like, and how you can compensate for each other or tolerate each other. This takes time and involves dialogue, challenges, and instances of frustration.

Know the criteria to choose your partner

In today's world there is a natural tendency to go after what is seen and felt. But the search for a partner requires more profound study. Love, inner beauty, character, emotional stability, attitude, goals, aspirations, values, priorities, honesty, talents, and communication are among the attributes that may help the relationship to sustain the various challenges of a family life. These are not obvious with a casual and quick encounter. You will learn more about each other, and this is often through trials and challenges.

Nurture your love

Love needs to be nurtured. The ingredients that can nurture it include vulnerability, humility, self-denial, responsibility, communication, and mutual respect. Learn to develop friendship along with your love, to enjoy each other's company. Develop your marriage rituals: embrace each other daily, e-mail, call, and talk to each other every day, even, or especially, when you are apart. Reserve time together. Remember important dates, such as birthdays and anniversaries. Work as a team; share plans, projects, and vacations. Treat each other with respect, and work together toward a long-lasting relationship. Have the time to laugh and play together. Show commitment and learn to manage crises together without blaming each other. Establish mutually agreed family structure, rituals, and a money management strategy. Treat each other as friends and not mere business partners, competing against each other. Provide a confident, proper environment for growth, spontaneity, and a mutual sense of well-being.

My maternal grandmother told me many stories; however, she never told me whether they were true or not.

In a lovely village, there was a gigantic piece of rock that hundreds of men could not move. It was a landmark to identify the village. Way above the rock, there was a small drip of water that was constantly dribbling one drop of water at a time in the middle of the rock. No one paid it any mind; it was less than insignificant. Ages passed, people came and went admiring the rock, completely unaware of the dripping water. One time, some elderly people pointed out that drops of water were digging a hole. Most people paid them no mind and went their way. Then, one day the whole village was horrified to see a big crack surrounding the rock, as if to break that unbreakable rock. It was a shock! But it was too late.

In the Song of Songs, Solomon says, to beware of "the little foxes that spoil the vines" No matter how big and strong love is in a relationship, never take it for granted. Never let the small things—the constant drip—eat away at it. Instead, tend it and nurture it like a beautiful bed of flowers.

Bad habits left unchecked can take a large toll on any relationship. A responsible couple spends time getting to know each other; they harmonize their convictions and priorities and learn steps to ventilate their frustrations. If you know you are in charge of your own happiness and manage to do your best to make your partner happy, then the battle is already half won. To make your partner happy, you must actively decide to be happy yourself. A mature couple always keeps open the channels of communication. Your partner may not require that much to be happy; a little understanding, attention, consideration, and acceptance will lubricate the engine for long mileage. Once you are committed to each other, it takes a full investment of all that you have to make it.

Identify And Try To Meet Your Partner's Needs

Physical needs

As responsible partners, you must both contribute to feeding, clothing, and lodging your family and try to make their lives as comfortable as possible. Someone who is lazy, selfish, drunk, and unable to hold a job or play his expected role in caring for his family is not worthy of being married. A couple may decide to have one person at home while the other works or they may decide to have both working. As long as it is by mutual agreement, there should be no problem. The difficulty arises when one partner is killing himself or herself while the other does not do the bare minimum, even at home. Sooner or later, the situation is bound to explode.

Sexual needs

When two people get married, sexual satisfaction is part of the package. If someone wants to take a woman as his wife, he must make sure he is virile enough to handle her sexually. The woman also must be willing and able to play her role. Intimate relationships have various levels that should not be taken lightly. Making love involves a few factors besides just mating. Falling in love and making love includes caressing, cuddling, and a lot of sweet nothings. Lovemaking also includes the willingness to accommodate and the fondness for the anticipation of the partner's needs, which may not always be expressed. A woman loves to be treated with respect, care, and tact. She wants to know that she is loved and desired. She is more than willing to spend the night in the arms of someone who can play the love symphony with her in one accord. Many unions have a short life span because the man proves to be rude and clumsy. These men get close to their partners only when they have the urge to satisfy their personal physiological needs. Even then, the act is dry, cold, and quick. Guys! Please put some oil and spice into your intimate experiences. We are not simple carriers of gametes. Any man who wants to maintain a romantic union must not only pay attention to his actions in the bedroom, but he must also pay attention to the way he treats his partner during the regular hours outside the bedroom. The woman also needs to remain attractive, committed to a harmonious relationship, and concerned about mutual sexual fulfillment. Again, the way you treat your partner daily affects the participation at night.

Emotional needs

Each partner must pay attention to the other's emotional well-being. Throughout the vicissitudes of life, during moments of anguish and anxiety, everyone needs someone to count on, someone to share concerns, someone who is interested in his or her activities. When the channels of communication are kept open, the level of frustration diminishes considerably. Little unexpected treats, like taking a walk together, holding hands, going to dinner or a movie, cement the love that you share.

The responsible woman strives to share the dreams of her husband, instead of shooting his dreams down one by one while reminding him of his past failures. She also takes time to speak to him and cheer him up when needed. Very few men like a quarrelsome, dirty, lazy, and aggressive woman, with vulgar manners and a foul mouth. Most men long for a charming, elegant, beautiful, and well-mannered companion. Her smile is like the first rays of the sun that disintegrate all the clouds in his sky. Her beauty is an everlasting, attractive perfume. Her voice sounds like an angelical concert that takes him to the third heaven. Regardless of her skills, talents, profession, and socio-cultural background, once she is married, she supports the goals of her partner, and together they walk toward fulfilling the common dreams of their home. A balanced home seeks the common success of the couple. They navigate together in the stormy sea of this troubled world. They find their formula to work out differences without attacking and morally or emotionally destroying each other. There is a common determination to make the relationship work, to build on it, and (if need be) to raise a family. No one wants to sleep with an everlasting competitor.

Healthy emotions and well-balanced sensibilities are important parameters for a successful marriage. When you consider that two strangers with generally different origins, orientations, educations, philosophies, family backgrounds, and characters get together to live harmoniously under the same roof, it requires more than sheer luck for them to make it through. Personal maturity, self-confidence, and self-respect are paramount to pursuing common goals. Love is a delicate plant that requires constant and systematic care. During the early moments together, each partner needs to learn about the other, while expressing their dreams, ideals, career aspirations, and worries. Make a habit of discussing those issues that are important to both parties by working on the network of communication. Honesty, determination, and respect will help cement the love you share. You have to establish a real commitment to stay together.

If you were not aware of them before, you will soon discover the key differences between the sexes. The man sees the forest as a whole, while the woman cares about every single branch of every single tree. If the former is after the ultimate result, the latter takes into account all the steps, the ways and means to reach the end result. A woman wants unconditional love from her partner. She wants his time, his undivided attention, his kindness, affection, gallantry, etc. She expects flowers, gifts, trips, nights out, romantic evenings, special weekends, and vacations. She wants quality and quantity time to be invested in her and their children. Best of all, she knows she deserves it; yet she is not likely to verbally request it.

Alas! So many men enjoy time with friends watching sports. So many invest their entire lives working 24/7 to provide everything under the sun for their families, thinking that they will have time later in life for their significant others. Unfortunately, they either never have that time or their family and partner are no longer there when they do! When the heart has been hurt, sacked, and tormented for so long by so many missed opportunities, it is really hard for that heart to mend; it may be irreparable. Time spent away to pursue material goals may not be compensated for later in sickness or when death makes them part. There will be somber times, times of failure, disappointment, and rejection. When the only one to stand by you was never truly appreciated, that is truly a missed opportunity!

Beware of Marriage Stressors

Experience has proved that certain factors and situations can affect the survival of any marriage. Besides character and personality, they include: changes in health, separation, raising children, change in employment, aging, empty nest syndrome, financial difficulties, imprisonment, addiction, and so forth.

The Pathway Toward Divorce (Avoid It!)

Nearly half of all marriages end in divorce. Why? Experience, observation, and available data point out key factors that seem to torpedo married life. These are: finances, incompatibility of character, and unfaithfulness.

Finances

To live you must be able to care for yourself and meet basic needs. When you fall in love initially, you live in the clouds, you dream, you are happy, and your emotions are high. That overwhelming sensation of feeling so good leaves almost no room to think about food. But once you are married, you settle down, and the reality of life sets in. You must face your responsibilities together. The time when your emotions are high and your heads are in the clouds with happy dreams no longer matches reality, and you must find a temporary position or a definite profession to earn a living and pay the bills. Your basic responsibilities may increase and your source of revenue may be limited. Economic stress can make you tense, irritable, and frustrated; if you're not careful, the situation may bring out the worse in everyone. Then the accusations, the blame game, the reproaches, and even a competitive attitude arrive. The result can be a rushed decision to get away from each other and seek a divorce. It takes a lot of maturity to face challenges together. Happy is the couple that has enough wisdom to identify the situation as a challenge, instead of venting out and dumping all the blame on the other partner. Such a condition requires good common sense, a clear determination to find a way out, and an agreement on what is absolutely necessary and what is optional. Many couples have gone through dark moments, but their commitment to stay the course allowed them to emerge with a healthier relationship. Adversities can either make you stronger and better or break you. The married life requires constant vigilance. Countless couples have sailed through severe storms together, then they become lax; they lie back and put down their guard. They slowly start to drift away from each other until they find themselves in high seas that crush their financial boat, and in despair they call it quits. Beware of financial infidelity. Do not mortgage the couple's future, the family's long term revenue by engaging in high risk transactions or reckless behavior. Such financial unfaithfulness can erode all trusts and torpedo the relationship.

Character incompatibility

Why do two people with their own personal bags of shortcomings, with their different backgrounds and genetic makeup, choose to live together "for better or for worse"? Take the time to know each other, learn about your pasts, your families, your values, and your beliefs. A child who grows up in a home where the father never fulfills his obligation as a father figure, where the mother is physically or emotionally abusive or abused, where alcohol or other stimulants are pulling the strings, where the parents are always quarrelling, where the house is unclean and upside-down, will likely grow up with scars that mark him for life. When he grows up he may have real difficulties living with someone whose childhood was spent in a functional, well-structured home. The lifestyle of the parents usually gives an idea of a person's future ability as a husband or wife.

Other triggers for disaster include getting married to become emancipated, or because of premature or unexpected pregnancy, a supposedly ticking biological clock, a harsh financial situation, or to show friends and family members that they too can get married. Unless the union is motivated by an unselfish love, a desire to love and cherish the partner, the steps in front of the altar are bound to fail. If things do not look good before marriage, there is no guarantee they will get better after. Things may even get worse. Do not marry someone with the hopes of molding them into someone of your own liking. After the union, the mask is usually thrown away, the truth is revealed, and it may not be pleasant. The reality is not often a pretty or an improved picture of what the appearances were before marriage. All in all, if you have serious doubts before you contract a marriage with someone, if there are certain features or character flaws that you cannot stand, then run while you are ahead of the game. Otherwise, you will probably feel deceived and will live a nightmare.

Unfaithfulness

In today's world, you spend long hours at work, either in your office or traveling and meeting people. Business takes you away from your family, and you spend a lot of time with friends and colleagues in your respective fields. You may find coworkers who are attractive, or who exhibit some qualities, some gifts, even certain characteristic attributes that you have longed to find in your own partner at home. The situation becomes even more precarious when the spouse at home has been there for a while and is getting old, shows contempt, talks a lot, criticizes a lot, demands too much, is never satisfied, is not appreciative, puts you down, and even occasionally disrespects you. At work, you meet someone who is always understanding and nice to you, who treats you well, encourages you, and shares your interests, someone who exhibits all the characteristics you wish your spouse at home would reveal. At home you are nothing, a nobody to accuse, disturb, confront, and attempt to boss around. At work, you are a little king or queen in Paradise Island. Slowly but surely an innocent friendship starts to develop at work. You start comparing your spouse with that innocent friend who has become the joy of your life. You begin to talk. The dialogue becomes more and more interesting. Slowly but surely, you enjoy going to work more than you enjoy going home. You spend some time together as friends, you eat lunch together, and soon you may even go to dinner together. You may stay late to work on a few projects together. You have a lot in common. Be careful! Unless this friendship cools down or the spouse at home gets a wake-up call, something physical is bound to happen.

You may have spent years and years to build up your home with a spouse and children, and alas, one moment of weakness blows it all away. No one is invulnerable. You cannot guarantee that your behavior is always going to be perfect. It all depends on the time, the circumstances, and the person who is sharing your company at that moment.

We are living in a permissive world. If you have no moral conviction, no ethical code of behavior, if there is no absolute truth, unfaithfulness triumphs. It is so glamorous; it is almost part of being successful. When you get married with a liberal philosophy of sharing your bed with other partners, your home will suffer enormously, and the outcome is likely to be dismal. In a marriage, the spouses must support each other. Let no partner push the other to the brink of unfaithfulness. Some behavior may make someone vulnerable: leaving your spouse alone all the time, failing to take care of emotional and sexual needs, mistreatment, disrespect, and so forth. By the same token, let no one look for excuses to live a loose life and sleep around with the illusion of impunity. This can lead straight to divorce. The assets are split, and the innocent children become traumatized victims.

People often ask me: What do you do if one partner is found to be unfaithful? This is a loaded question. The answer depends on the couple and the couple alone. Love conquers all; however, the guilty partner must confess, repent, and show new and improved behavioral patterns. Forgiveness requires giving up the bad habits and abandoning the environment that facilitates such behavior. To deserve forgiveness, you must show true repentance, with no alibi, no explanations or excuses to justify reprehensible behavior. Unless you knew you were getting married to a popular "not enough to go around" partner, who is always after adventures, you cannot knowingly accept certain behavior. People do not change overnight; this is why, before you tie the knot with a Don Juan macho man, you need some time to follow him. If a lady feels she can accommodate friends as she pleases, you must think before you say, "I do." If you seek forgiveness, you must be willing to forgive the other partner who has committed some indiscretion as well. It cannot be an ongoing pattern of behavior.

Sexual dissatisfaction

Sexual relations are a well-deserved delight for every couple. Before getting into it, you should acquire as much knowledge as possible. Sexual relationships require a physical and emotional maturity. Without that, the adverse consequences of intimate sexual relationships can last throughout life. You can wind up with an unwanted pregnancy, sexually-transmitted disease, AIDS, and a long list of unexpected mental, physical, spiritual, and socio-cultural aftermaths that mark your life forever.

Sex affects everyone and pervades our culture. The little girl is dressed up and getting ready to go to a friend's party, when she suddenly turns to her mother and says, "Mama, am I sexy?" Sexual relations are no longer a privilege shared by two committed people. Regardless of culture, beliefs, or religious orientation, everyone has sexual urges, and few people want to wait to find the appropriate time, place, and person with whom to express them. Sexual intimacy is not an end by itself but a means to renew the couple's commitment to each other, and these relations should be unique and personal. Sex is not taboo for a well-balanced couple; it is a precious gift to be enjoyed fully. It is even one of the key elements that contribute to the success and the fulfillment of marriage.

One afternoon a couple comes in to ask for some help. The wife says, "I am tired of him cheating on our mutual arrangement." When asked what type of arrangement the couple had, she replies, "We agreed to have sex only on Sunday and Wednesday night, and he keeps asking for more."

What a shock! Sex is something to enjoy mutually; it cannot be part of a rigid context or an obligatory schedule. Anytime you or your partner has to request a specific schedule to have intimate relations with the other, this is a sign that there are bigger problems. If one of you does not enjoy sex, find out why. You may need professional advice in the form of a few therapy sessions together. If your overall relationship is doing fine, the question of how often, when, and where does not come up. Of course, you have to have the proper milieu, time, and mental and physical preparedness. After being rude, selfish, and antagonistic all day, if one partner decides to initiate a sexual approach at night—even when the other partner yields to the request, it is likely to be mechanical. A sulking woman, who loves to complain, is careless, neglectful, and aggressive, is likely to rub out all enthusiasm and excitement for a lovely evening. Likewise, a man who is rude, inconsiderate, lazy, violent, and careless does not make it easy for a partner who has struggled all day to make ends meet. A busy schedule, the type and amount of work, sickness, worries, and various other sources of stress can affect a sexual relationship. Physical and psychological preparation and readiness do contribute to the success of such relations.

The bottom line is to make time to foster love. When the moment comes, it may require the proper ambiance, scenery, music, patience, and calm. Above all, love requires time and know-how. You do not make love by a stopwatch or while watching TV or answering the telephone. Do not neglect the preliminaries—sweet dialogue, soft touches, and affectionate kisses. A little massage here and there, unexpected, pleasant, passionate moves, exploring your partner's body and stimulating sensitive spots, all play a role in ultimate success.

Even penetration must be carefully done for the enjoyment and the surprise of your partner. This is not a football game or a boxing match. The love adventure must be mutually pursued and won. Often, your partner will set a desired rhythm, which depends on the passionate flame, physical well-being, frame of mind, and the time and circumstances. If the woman is nervous, fanciful, and challenging, she may ask for a strong, virile physical performance. Other times, she may want a rhythmical, harmonious waltz. The man must be gallant and understanding, with the unique goal to be irreplaceable or at least memorable. (Ladies, do not be too capricious or too prudish to show or tell your lover what is exciting and pleasurable.)

There is also a way of finishing. Do not just pull out and turn around to go to sleep, or get dressed to go and do other things. You are not a hunter who can rush out of the forest once he gets his prey. Again, time is of the essence. It is the moment to caress, cuddle, sweet talk, and remain intertwined for a while. Some partners love to sleep in the arms of their mate.

Some people wonder whether they should regularly experience an orgasm during sexual intercourse. It would be ideal to do so. However, it is not always possible, because of factors including time, place, physical and emotional predisposition, mental preparedness, and overall performance and duration. If it hardly ever happens, then the couple must investigate to identify the cause. There are instances when the help of an expert may be required. At any rate, you must avoid monotony and selfishness. You must know when it is mutually feasible, and you should learn not to force yourself onto your partner. Avoid those failed quick, repeated mini-sessions that you engage in just to keep your partner happy. Avoid faking it, because sooner or later, you will be discovered, and the impact may go beyond what you might have expected. An appropriate session requires time, participation, and satisfaction of both partners. Do not let you or your partner make it a habit of just doing it for the sake of fulfilling a contract. It should be as mutually enjoyable and sought after by you as it is by your mate. Otherwise, you must find out why. The experienced hunter does not pull out his rifle just to shoot at anything that moves.

Other Factors That May Destroy A Home

There are other factors that affect the welfare of a home and unfortunately wind up increasing the number of divorces in our world. Besides incurable disease and unwanted pregnancy, they include constant criticism, baseless jealousy, disrespect and eagerness to fight, constant arguing, verbal or physical abuse, silence, and ignoring your partner's feelings and needs. The tendency to always be right, to always win every argument, to always have the last word, while minimizing or ignoring your partner's input or concerns, is one way of communicating "my way!"

A seldom discussed condition is infertility. People take for granted the possibility of giving birth to a healthy baby who brings joy and delight to a family. But many couples would move heaven and earth to have a child. When a couple spends one or more years trying vainly to begin a pregnancy, the stress keeps rising. Infertility affects both the man and the woman in the relationship, and both must seek medical treatment.

Many factors can result in infertility, including heredity, physiological incompatibility, anatomical variations, age, low sperm count, and morphology. Infertility remains a personal and intimate problem. If you are fertile, show enough consideration not to embarrass those who are not. When a couple spends quite some time together without children, do not put them on the spot with embarrassing questions. Be tactful and supportive. Do not make them feel handicapped or unfulfilled as a family. They have enough stress, frustration, and unanswered questions; do not add to their burden. Often, financial restraints, religious beliefs, moral values, ethics, or other personal issues limit their choices. Some go on to adopt, while others continue to hope. Whatever the case, do not make them feel guilty. You can only be responsible for your own actions, not theirs. We are not responsible for that which does not depend on us.

Parents and Children

Giving birth to a baby is one of the most delightful and important events in life, especially when it is the first time from a willing mother. But wait! Before you reach that stage, it generally takes nine months between the day of conception and the time of birth. What a long period! The mother's body undergoes all kinds of changes, to suit the embryo that becomes the fetus and to allow the formation of the different organs and the harmonization of all the functions, in order to bring out a beautiful and healthy baby.

But beware! Raising a child is not like raising a garden plant in the backyard. A well-balanced home welcomes the baby with fascinations. In that home, the relationship between the parents on the one hand and the rapport between the parents and the baby on the other hand will determine the life of the baby in more ways than one. If the baby grows up in a family with a relaxed atmosphere and sane surroundings, where he can develop steadily without unpredictable interruption, he has a greater chance of becoming a steady, reliable, and mature person. Education begins in the cradle. The child learns very early to imitate and follow his parents. While growing up, he will differ from his siblings and reveal a character and temperament that are likely to be unique. The parents must see eye-to-eye regarding his upbringing. If he can differentiate between their strengths and approaches toward him, then he learns to manipulate that difference. The parents must share the common goal of preparing an honest, disciplined, reliable, and loyal citizen. From childhood through adolescence, parents must show integrity and firmness. To leave the child to raise himself and do whatever he or she wants is a sure route toward disaster. Parents must not be cowardly, irresponsible, or abusive; a child needs supervision and guidance. The parents must show love, provide time, and always be available to lead the proper way.

When parents act as friends, their children will less likely hesitate to come to them for advice about various subjects such as drugs, sex, contraceptives, and alcohol. Parents must always be willing to help and encourage their children. Children need parental input in the selection of their friends, habits, hobbies, music, movies, clothing, and even eating habits. The dialogue must start early. The child needs to develop autonomy and self-confidence while under his parents' supervision. Parents and children must not confuse love with tolerance, indulgence, or negligence. For a child to grow harmoniously, he must know boundaries, what is right or wrong, what is acceptable and what is not acceptable.

A proactive approach to parenting is commendable. Life is made up of choices, and we must be ready to pay the price for every choice we make. The child must know the role he plays in the home and start to behave responsibly as soon as possible. The spoiled child goes straight down the path of deception. The world may see this child as lazy, rebellious, and even criminal. Bad habits come in clusters, and friends are often the source that condones them. That is why parents must be vigilant and proactive in creating a healthy relationship with their children. The best influence on a child is the good example seen in the life of the parents. A home where the parents appreciate the spirit of service, morality, a sense of responsibility, obedience, kindness, temperance, a sense of humor, love for beautiful things, and moral values, plants seeds that hopefully the children will internalize and practice themselves. A lasting marriage, as well as the children's education, cannot be left at the mercy of luck. Intellectual, physical, moral, and socio-economic well-being require hard work. Because, even after the parents go through all those steps, they still run the risk of their children shying away from the drafted path. This is another reason why parents must do all their best to raise their children the right way, so that they will not have a guilty conscience if ever things turn sour.

With the globalization of culture and the proliferation of new technologies, today's youth live in a world that is different from the one their parents grew up in. Everything is being redefined, including truth, family, morality, and ethics. No matter what, parents must hold the standards and pass them on. They must teach the new generation the basic tools to distinguish between right and wrong, true and false, good and bad. There seems to be a shock and a cultural clash between the generations, or even a tendency toward confrontation. A dialogue, a practical approach, and a compromise is necessary.

These children are often molded by television, Internet, cyberspace, iPods, cell phones, and peer pressure. The norms are fuzzy and suggestive. There is almost no solid structure until they do something awful that shocks everybody; until then they are mostly ignored. Parents are busy working several jobs to make ends meet and provide whatever is necessary for their children. Parents are pulled in many directions. They worry about their financial situation, their ability to meet their own needs and those of their offspring. They have personal and emotional issues. They think about job security, furthering their education, health issues, eventual retirement, sick and dependent parents, housing, etc. How many of their children will end up going to university? Even when they do, will they be able to afford it? While trying to deal with all these questions and many more, the children are growing and dealing with their own pressing issues. The time available for dialogue and interaction with their parents is reduced. Anger, frustration, misunderstanding, and even mistrust develop on both sides. Unfortunately, many parents only intervene when things go wrong, or they intervene too briefly and the loving message does not get through or is misinterpreted. The words used may have different meanings to different groups.

How many parents long to share the good moments with their kids, like in a sport or a school performance, yet they are struggling to make ends meet? The children are often too young to understand why; they may become upset and resentful. This may result in negative changes in their behavior. Some adolescents are anxious and misunderstood. They need and they seek love and acceptance. A peculiar and strained relationship can develop between parents and children, but there is no reason to despair. Everyone needs to do his share for the community. The younger generation is going through some phases. The parents are doing the best they know how to survive in these current circumstances. Therefore, both sides can continue with love, understanding, forgiveness, and discipline. You can rearrange your priorities; take time to talk to each other with respect, without jumping to conclusions or passing judgment. You need to accept each other as you are, instead of trying to make others the way you want them to be.

You can travel the road together, developing a close relationship between the old and the new generation. With the spirit of forgiveness, identify the different challenges of the youth: identity crisis, peer pressure, exposure to narcotics, etc. Refrain from condemnation. You should tell them and show them that you love them unconditionally instead. You can spend some time with them while it is not too late; do whatever is humanly possible to improve on the relationship.

You must be perfectible, willing to learn from others, to correct the mistakes, repair what is repairable and improve the home, the relationships, and yourself continuously. This is the way to be successful. A man has his role to play, a woman has hers, and so do the children. When everyone plays his or her part, the orchestra can play a lovely symphony.

Man	Woman
• Pay undivided attention to your spouse	• Encourage your husband
• Tell her often how much you love her	• Be his devoted companion
• Give her well-deserved quality time	• Respect and congratulate him
• Bring her surprises, souvenirs	• Tell him you love him
• Do not waste her money	• Do not antagonize him
• Stay away from laziness	• Accept him as he is
• Learn how to control yourself	• Do your best to please him

Profile of an Ideal Family

Parents	Children
• Show unconditional love	• Find your roles and responsibilities
• Cultivate happy relationships	• Carry out your assigned duties
• Set the fields for understanding	• Cultivate good manners
• Keep the line of communication open	• Do not follow the crowd
• Be tactful, firm, and diligent	• Resist peer pressures
• Be slow to judge and prompt to congratulate	• Be a conciliator
• Be an available friend always	• Remember that parents have good intentions

Parents remember, your main goal is to act as a guide, a facilitator, to help them get through childhood and be there for them. Please love them even when they do not deserve it. They need it. A chapter on love and family that ignores the single-parent home is incomplete. In America, Europe, and other parts of the world, countless children are being raised by one parent. There are many causes, such as divorce and separation, the decision not to marry, and the death of one parent. There are a few factors that contribute throughout the world to the situation, including cultural, social, and economic changes. An increasing number of children grow up in a home where one parent carries all the burdens that were already too much for two. There is an impact on both the single person and the children. The challenges include financial difficulties, housing, child care, health care, emotional support, job training, youth activities, and more. This represents a real challenge to find an adequate coping mechanism to fill in the gaps and alleviate the burdens and the stress for both the parent and the child. Regardless of the causes, some steps must be taken to deal with the situation. The single parent must be determined to continue the course while doing his or her best. As a child of a single parent myself, I can recall my mother's resources for dealing with single-parenthood. She refused to feel sorry for herself and did not want to blame herself for the situation. She kept her head straight, remained positive, and held no grudges. She always assured me of her love. Very early, she provided a structured environment, made me get involved in the decision-making at home, taught me to do well in school, to stay out of trouble, and to be responsible and disciplined, while remaining a child and enjoying my childhood. She showed discipline in her financial life, teaching me the difference between wants and needs. I could always approach her about anything at any time. Every now and then she would take some time for herself, look after herself, and meet with some other women in the neighborhood to talk and laugh. Somehow, I feel fortunate to have had such a close relationship with her, to learn early the ways of life without losing my childhood. She knew how to turn a situation around while reminding me: when you are dealt a situation, the trick is in how you react to it and cope with it. Society in general, the community as well as friends, grandparents, and religious and community-based organizations can provide that extra support needed to face difficult issues. There are single-parent resource networks available that help to find an efficient approach to level out the playing field and develop programs and projects to make it feasible for both parents and children.

Throughout the stormy seas that are devouring this world, the home must be a sure anchor for the family unit. A well-balanced and stable home is the best nest to form and mend solid characters for life. Family success is paramount for the optimal success. Home is the base, the spine, and the framework on which rests a viable society. Show me your family and your home, and I will then have an idea of your community and your current and future society.

Health and Success

Ingredients For a Healthy Life

If the quantity of life is important, so should be the quality. Reconsider a simpler way of living. A healthy life that is full of energy and joy depends on some basic ingredients. Here are ten keys to a healthy life:

1. Water

Water is the source of life. No one can survive beyond a few days without water. About eighty percent of your blood, sixty percent of your body, seventy-five percent of your brain is made up of water. Without adequate water, the blood becomes more concentrated and circulation diminishes. The body then lacks oxygen and other elements, loses its capacity to get rid of toxins, and malfunctions in various ways. The brain gets less oxygen and glucose. The entire body starts to decompose. Drink a decent amount of water daily to maintain equilibrium. Other drinks, such as juice, soda, or alcohol, do not replace plain, clean water. Be aware of the quality of the water you drink. Public water supplies vary in quality, but if your local government certifies its potability, it should be safe to drink. Some people prefer bottled water or they install a water filter.

2. Air

Air is essential for life. Learn to breathe in deeply through your nose and exhale completely through your mouth. Get outside in an unpolluted place and enjoy the fresh air with regular long walks.

3. Food

You need a well-balanced diet with a variety of nutrients. The key is to select a variety of foods that can maintain your health by providing enough energy, as well as the essentials needed for structural build-up and repair and well-balanced functioning of your cells and tissues. Take the time to eat slowly and at regular set times. Beware of chemical contamination and consumption. You are what you eat.

4. Sun

The sun's rays provide energy, heat, light, and purification to the planet. Lack of sunlight can affect some people's mood, especially during autumn and winter. You need some natural sunlight to help your body stay healthy, but you need to protect yourself against overexposure to the sun, as that can result in skin cancer in later life.

5. Rest

Not long ago, it was reported that a midday rest may be good for you, good for your heart. Why not? Physical and mental rest is indispensable to maintain your equilibrium. It is conducive toward better health, improves moods, creates a stronger immune system, and increases productivity. If you are constantly working and are always on edge, you become more accident-prone, nervous, irritable, and even dangerous to yourself and others. A good night's sleep helps you to regain your energy, stay young, and prolong your life span. You need to develop the habit of going to bed at a regular hour and getting adequate hours to sleep. The exact number depends on the individual. But reasonably, an average of six hours daily should be the minimum. Sleep and rest must be part of your daily agenda. It is not an option.

6.   Physical exercise

You have heard it before. Here it is again. Get off the couch and exercise. A sedentary, passive, comfortable life can hurt you physically. Using elevators, cars, electrical stairs, and remote controls must not stop you from getting regular exercise. I know people whose best exercise consists of sitting down and watching others on TV play sports. They buy all kinds of equipment for possible exercise, yet even the treadmill becomes nothing more than an expensive clothes hanger. You owe it to yourself to start being more active and stay active; you will be glad you did, as it will help you to age gracefully in later life.

7.   Cleanliness

Cleanliness is universally appreciated and attainable by all. It provides a restful and healthy environment. It gives joy, peace, and respect to its practitioners. If you have to choose between a dirty yet sumptuous palace with the best furniture and appliances on earth and a thatched cottage clean and well maintained, you should go for the latter. Cleanliness is the mirror of your character, the reflection of your soul. Although it may seem unfair, a quick visit to someone's house can give you an idea of who he is. A house should always be clean, especially the living room, the kitchen, and the bathroom. You should never confuse being clean with being wealthy.

8.   Recreation

One of the ways to remain well-balanced is to find time to enjoy life. If you keep on going 24/7, there will come a time when you will crash. Sickness should not be the only reason to stop going. You need time to go on vacation, to engage in different and enjoyable activities. Once in a while, you deserve to take the load off your brain, your back, and your feet. Even a brand new car needs to be serviced regularly to remain fully efficient. The human being needs a tune-up now and then, too. Recreation is the main tool to regain vigor and vitality and to replenish your energy to pass to a higher level. Remember, you can live without money, but without your life you cannot enjoy what money can provide. So live within your means and take time to smell the roses, to enjoy that one life you have, to spend time with yourself, your family members, your children, your grandchildren, your friends, and any loved ones. You need it. You deserve it.

9.   Stress management

The modern world has made stress an omnipresent companion, if not the master of everyone's life. Be it at home, in the workplace, on the road, stress is eating you alive. Although a minimum of stress is good for you, as it enables you to perform well, the constant flow of stress is unhealthy. Your body reacts the same to stress, regardless of its source. Too many mental, physical, and emotional stimuli at a constant rate wind up having a deleterious impact on you. The reaction to stress is unique in every person. Stress can cause irritability, insomnia, migraines, pain, change in appetite, malaise, fatigue, and further pathology, such as depression and weakening of the immune system. Stress affects the brain and the heart. To deal with the various stressors, you need to take the following steps:

- Acknowledge their existence.
- Identify the cause.
- Beware of unidentified or hidden causes.
- Recognize the symptoms.

- Deal with stress diligently.

- Develop proper strategies: water intake, exercise, massage, swimming, biking, ball playing, cleanliness, harmony, a balanced life.

- Make a conscious effort to minimize stress.

10. Service and spirituality

It is healthy to have a purposeful life, to know that you can make the difference in other people's lives. When you know you are needed, appreciated, respected for being useful, empathic; when you maintain community relationships and contribute to others' well-being, you benefit from a certain satisfaction, joy, and peace that contribute to your own well-being. And if everything else fails, you can rely on your trust and your faith that provide hope and optimism; that also positively affects your health overall.

Steps Toward a Better Life

One of the main causes of the world's unhealthy condition is the quality of the food, the environment, and the lifestyle. So what is the solution?

Do we rush into a special crash diet for seven to ten days? Do we walk around with a mask to breathe, or do we all start walking miles back and forth to be in good shape. Obviously, this is not feasible. So what must we do?

Develop healthy eating habits that include eating the proper amount at the right time; stop nibbling every five minutes. Get into the habit of eating properly most of the time, stay active, and let your weight take care of itself. Some people really have a weight problem that requires special guidance, counseling, and even a specialist's intervention; but many of us just need to discipline ourselves and control our attraction toward food. How many times have we eaten just because the food was available?

1. Avoid refined and processed foods that are laced with artificial ingredients, chemicals, and preservatives. Learn to prepare and enjoy simple meals with a limited amount of salt, sugars, and overly spicy ingredients. Use unrefined starchy foods that are naturally high in fiber and low in fat, such as dark yellow and green leafy vegetables, fresh whole fruits, legumes, salads, whole wheat, brown rice, wild rice, yams, squash, potatoes, whole grain products, and natural cereals with no sugar added. The refrain remains: eat more fruit and vegetables. As a matter of fact, such a diet positively affects your health. It lowers your risk for heart disease, stroke, cancer, diabetes, and hypertension. It also helps in vascular function and weight loss. With the proper intake of vitamins, minerals, and proteins, some now advise a vegan diet. Even a flexible diet, with a mixture of fruits, vegetables, nuts, beans, lean meat, and low-fat dairy products, is considered appropriate. The bottom line is this: there is enough variety to attract everyone toward a healthy diet and nutrition.

2. Watch what you buy, how you cook it, how readily available it is, and the amount of time you take to eat it. Watch what you drink and watch your dessert intake.

3. Refrain from neutralizing the great diet effort by adding things such as salad dressing, mayonnaise, butter, gravy, and readily accessible salt and sugar on the table. Low-trans-fat margarines or oils (if you

have to use some flavor enhancers, especially for the beginners) are recommended.

4. Have a solid, well-balanced breakfast (fruits, low- or no-sugar cereals, juice, low-fat or skim milk). When in a real rush, grab a banana or an apple.

5. Drink plenty of water.

6. Cultivate a positive attitude and learn to enjoy every minute of life.

7. Avoid eating late at night and right before bed.

8. Remember that water is better than juice.

9. Resist giving up after one or two faux pas. Do not be so punitive of yourself that you give up after you come up short; keep trying.

10. Carry healthy snacks with you for unexpectedly long hours at work.

11. Know what your ideal weight should be, while taking into account your own individuality.

There is no way you can go back or continue the same pathway toward destruction. You want to live and enjoy an excellent quality of life. If the number of years you live is important to you, its quality also should be important. As a lucid and intelligent person, you must take inventory of your life; it is worth reviewing the basic, simple notions of health.

Prevention is important to your health. Health maintenance, together with screening for early detection of any potential illnesses, represents the wise approach. Some simple steps are to keep warm in the wintertime; avoid excess heat in the summertime; and be wary of allergy seasons and possible allergic reactions to something you eat, inhale, or touch, or to some medications. Pay attention to your eyesight: How good is your vision? Have you noticed any changes lately? See your ophthalmologist at once and together determine the frequency of follow-up visits. Dental care: When was the last time you saw the dentist? Do not wait until you become symptomatic. Healthy teeth are important for your health. Remember your skin: Take good care of it and protect it by wearing appropriate clothing, avoiding sun exposure, using sunscreen, and cleansing regularly with the proper cleanser and moisturizer. Avoid health hazards and practice safety at all times.

Breathing fresh air, eating healthy natural foods, moderate exposure to the sun, taking time to rest, going on vacation, taking a walk, enjoying the elements of nature, exercising two to five times a week as clinically feasible, good oral and general hygiene, cleanliness, and the use of medications when properly prescribed are the main factors that contribute to a healthy lifestyle. Stay active, keep up with the good habits, and stay fit. Do the best you can; the rest does not depend on you.

Practical advice for men

Be healthy and stay healthy. A man over forty must have a regular, thorough physical exam, including a rectal examination, prostate evaluation, blood tests (blood count, glucose test, cholesterol, prostate, thyroid function test, electrolytes, urinalysis, and stools for blood), baseline EKG, blood pressure measurement, height and weight, glaucoma evaluation, colonoscopy, endoscopy, chest x-ray, and other tests possibly based on personal and family history and clinical presentation. The follow-up frequency depends on the findings and the decision between you and your doctor.

Practical advice for women

An annual check-up is a wise choice, especially if you are older than twenty-five or thirty. The annual evaluation should include a complete history and physical examination, Pap smear, blood pressure measurement, baseline blood tests to check for anemia, cholesterol, kidney function, urinalysis, and stools for blood. Based on age, complaint, and personal and family history, other tests may also include mammogram, colonoscopy, and endoscopy.

Do not neglect your mental and emotional condition. If you have such concerns, never hesitate to discuss them with a physician.

There is no foolproof, magical formula to guarantee a healthy and long life. However, the steps suggested above can certainly help you make it through. If you want a healthy life, learn to cultivate good habits, foster a positive attitude, seek some support group that will lift you up and not tear you down, frequent the gym, see your doctors regularly, and follow their advice. And remember the role of spirituality in health.

Poor health makes us irritable, troubled, and even desperate at times. Despite scientific advances, suffering because of illness remains high. The quantity and quality of life remains a priority for all. As a doctor, I classify people as follows:

- Those who are born healthy, yet fail to appreciate such a great gift until they no longer have it.

- Those who were born with shaky health and various on and off symptoms, but remain determined to make it, even when there may be no clear diagnosis or no known cure

- Those who develop chronic diseases and have to find strategies to live with them.

Regardless of the cause of illness, lack of health takes a heavy toll on a sick person, their environment, and community. Illness is costly economically, emotionally, and morally. Some conditions are unbearable, heartbreaking, untreatable, and unfair.

Do the best you can in your circumstances to maintain or improve your health. Remember these simple steps:

1. Take inventory of your health now. Be objective and base it on your age, sex, race, genetics, and environmental risks. Be ready, willing, and able to make lifestyle modifications. Everyone needs to modify the way he thinks, eats, and lives.

2. Identify the enemies of health, such as bad habits, overwork, stress, and emotional and situational constraints.

3. Evaluate your daily activities. You need at least six hours of sleep, a balanced diet, regular water intake, and regular exercise. Cultivate healthy, positive thoughts; rearrange your schedule for leisure time.

Remember to laugh, love, help, and hope; watch your posture, manage your time well, and keep a positive attitude. These are all excellent ways to help your entire being.

Spirituality and Success

Seeking to Define Religion

Every person who comes into this world, who hears, sees, smells, tastes, and touches, becomes curious and wants answers to many of life's questions. Very early on, a toddler's inquisitive mind leads him to wonder about almost everything. Why do we have days and nights? How come a big plane can fly like a bird, but I cannot? As he gets older, he is torn by many other questions. Why did grandpa die? Is there life after death? As he makes his way into adulthood, he wants to know more about the earth, the moon, the sun, the stars, the galaxies… where do these things come from? Were they specially designed or did they just come about?

Although the same brain pathways and mechanisms are more or less shared by all, the answers to all these questions, and many others, depend upon individual background, culture, environment, acquired knowledge— as well as the source of knowledge, the ability to face various challenges in life, and the eagerness to understand how things really come into existence. In their fascination with the mysteries of life, and in the struggle of facing many challenges, people naturally want to call upon a superior force or being. The direction they take depends on the answers postulated for all the enquiries. As time goes by, as knowledge increases, as man feels more secure and less intimidated by the unknown, he is able to recognize that there is an innate desire to live forever in his man-made paradise. This quest will lead him to come up with various hypotheses as to how to perpetuate himself and enjoy everlasting life. He becomes more and more curious. The more he is puzzled, the further he wants to venture on the odyssey of life. He quickly discovers that on the one hand, there is the visible world and the invisible world; on the other hand, he is limited in time and space. This does not deter him from his desire to know more about the human existence, his surroundings, and the functioning of the universe. Depending on developed beliefs, he becomes a god, a son of God, or a part of the whole. Whether he denies it or admits it, he is bound to seek a superior being or force. Deep inside of him, he believes in somebody or something. This belief directs his choices and his actions. This is how religions arise.

When we talk about success, we cannot ignore people's religious faith. Each time we speak about the origin of life and human destiny, religion lies in the background. It has always played a pivotal role, as life generally oscillates between hope and despair. Pulled between these two poles, our religious convictions determine our daily approach to life. When facing fear, anguish, crises, challenges, and trials, we tend to call upon a superior power to help us stay alive. In the absence of scientific understanding, man beseeched the gods to request special favors. The prayer was for rain when it was a dry hot season, for the sun when it rained too long, and for other miraculous interventions to meet the daily challenges of life. Then mankind becomes wiser. The more we learned about ourselves and the environment, the more we mastered the elements of nature. The more we benefited from scientific discoveries and technology, the more successful we became in our enterprises.

Our religion tended to become more sophisticated and our beliefs went through some modifications.

To avoid any misunderstandings, let me define what I mean by religion. Religion represents an ensemble of beliefs, values, practices, and activities that govern a human's life. It includes your conviction about the universe at large and about the human position and condition in particular.

Like most people, you may consciously tend to put religion at the lowest priority. Education, instruction, work, familial and parental relationships, health, career, socio-economic positions, and leisure time are all more important to you. Then, if there is time, you may think about religion; that is, you may recognize that there is a power above all that determines your destiny and to whom is required obedience and respect. Not everyone admits or believes this. Many ignore such a definition, or they even resent the idea of such a belief. Generally, we live according to our beliefs, and we evolve in harmony with our different credos. This explains why so many people run after a religion that is at the mercy of the believers' choices and unruly desires. The trend is toward a "one size fits all" religion where you can serve according to your own understanding of the concept of spirituality. Do you believe that every pathway leads to the same golden gates of heaven, if there is a heaven? Maybe you try to play it safe and appease your conscience by adopting a religion defined according to your tastes, your feelings, your understandings, your philosophy, and your viewpoint. So you choose to create or adapt your god according to your liking, a god that must be happy with the boundaries fixed by man and play the role he is assigned to play. The ontological and ecumenical aspects of the supreme divine are reduced into one single and common part. People spend their entire life self-righteously explaining God, while the fact of the matter is that God is beyond human explanation.

What happens after death? Does anyone really know? The true answer to that question does not depend on your ability to out-spin or outsmart others. It is not up to your own wisdom, understanding, emotions, or deductions.

Is there anything after death? Better yet, is there any possibility that there is something after death? Is God a reality or a mere invention of man's imagination? Although your answer does not change the reality of God, it does make a world of difference for your ultimate destiny. The existence of God does not depend on whether or not you love Him, respect Him, or adore Him. If God does not exist, whatever you do or say cannot make Him become real. The existence of a Supreme Being is not under your control, or at the mercy of your recognition or your decisions. Some people say that if you believe that God exists and He is good, it is all right for you. And if you believe that God does not exist, this is also fine. No one wants to go beyond such a compromised and ambiguous position. Unfortunately, as intelligent beings, our common sense says to take this issue a bit more seriously. After all, you know it is impossible to have two ideas in opposition to each other that are both true and right. One of the two is wrong, and only one can be right. The outcome is too important and crucial to leave it up to chance. Yet different beliefs coexist, each claiming to be the ultimate truth for its believers.

But it is not necessary to belong to a specific assembly to be religious. The sum of all the values that you have internalized all your life makes up your religion; this religion will determine your intellectual attitudes, your moral values, and the way you relate to others.

The Cartesian approach, available social models, the prowess of science and technology, and the impact of secularization lead many to question religious dogma. Some go so far as to state that religion can no longer provide unerring guidelines for human behavior, especially in the Western world. However, this postmodern, globalized world is full of problems, tragedies, dilemmas, and challenges. As more and more discoveries are made, more unanswered questions multiply. The more secure we feel, the more vulnerable we become. The more powerful and wealthy we are, the more we become a target for all kinds of evil. Success comes along with jealousy and hatred from our declared and undeclared enemies. The outcome is increased anxiety, increased insecurity, and increased worries. Remember, man acts or reacts according to the ambiance where he grows. If the environment is more toxic, you are likely to be more unpredictable and unstable. This takes us back to the question, is religion really outdated? Should it be completely abolished? Is it an obstacle to your success, or can it be a facilitator? In other words, is success incompatible with religion? Based on the initial definition of religion, it is an integral part of success. It can be a facilitator as well as a hindrance to success.

Religion has always had its role to play. The current period is no exception. Religion is a medium that eases the contact between man and the supernatural. It is a springboard to allow humans to succeed far beyond their visible limitations and pursue goals that aid in the improvement of self. Religion plays a role in the physical and psychological realms; it determines the limits of your explorations and defines the boundaries of your fears. It allows you to play on two keyboards together: the temporal and the everlasting. It gives you the strength to persevere, to develop new strategies, and to reach your goals. It is not an end in itself, but a means to reach your maximum potential.

In a world filled with pollution and all kinds of evil, a sure anchor, a superior force is needed to offer solutions to the various problems and challenges that plague this planet. True religion should seek the well-being of everyone and respect the differences in opinion and approaches. It should provide the tools necessary to progressively climb the ladder of success and the ability to help others. It should fight against pride, selfishness, exploitation, and injustice. It should enforce the concept that all human beings are created equal, with the inalienable rights to pursue happiness and freedom without prejudice to one's neighbor. Religion should convince everyone to be helpful to his neighbor in need, regardless of color, creed, or orientation.

Religion: Double-Edged Sword

Unfortunately, religion is one of the most misunderstood and misused concepts in the world.

- Many religions claim to know "the truth." How many truths can we have? Among those who use the same text (the Bible, for example), how can so many people come up with so many different interpretations? Even among Christians, there are different doctrines based on the same scriptures. In this era of globalization, the rituals and habits of each religion can no longer be a secret. A few extremists threaten the general population. The hidden agenda of many, the culture of hatred, even terrorist acts are committed in the name of religion. These mishaps definitely do not give credibility to such a concept.

- The behavior of some religious leaders is another sad chapter. A few discredit the faith; they talk loudly but do not practice what they preach. The real Master can easily say to them, "I never knew you." They prepare a heavy yoke and many burdens for the assembly, but they do not practice them themselves. They are a bunch of hypocrites, who do exactly the opposite of what they preach so loudly. It makes everyone wonder, and many are confused. It is all worth nothing, and we should all realize that man is not perfect, and religious leaders are humans. But they must account for their deeds.

- A deep consideration of religion can convince you that it has been the source of many wars. People want to kill each other in the name of religion; they call each other all kinds of names, such as "the great Satan," "the anti-Christ," "the axis of evil," and "the infidel." We become God's advocates and we decide on our own who to send to paradise and who to send to hell. God did not delegate such a prerogative to any human being. Is this the right attitude of a true believer?

Many people just get plain confused and discouraged. They decide that religion is a farce for the traitors who want to hide behind religion to take care of their affairs. To be fair, when you realize that adherence to one set of beliefs can lead people to act like robots who perform wicked acts, this is definitely more dangerous than just believing in nothing. Fanatical zeal based on a twisted interpretation of a given doctrine is as lethal as a loaded automatic firearm in the hands of a kid.

Depending on the credo and its interpretation, some religious organizations hold an immense power over their congregations. The impact of those beliefs within the community can go beyond the national boundaries. Here are some key factors that play a pivotal role in the destiny of a nation where religious tendencies are very strong:

- The period of civilization that dominates that religion—antiquity, the Middle Ages, the modern and postmodern eras.

- The level, the speed, and the amount of progress in scientific discoveries and their application, and their impact on that society.

- The current state of the culture and civilization.

- Sociological, geographic, educational, and economic conditions of the population at large, as well as individually.

The individual choice toward one assembly instead of another depends on:

- The biological and sociological milieu and familial background.

- The level of education and knowledge.

- Personal experiences and exposures.

- The impact of globalization, the awareness of other cultures and beliefs.

- The sociological and economical impact of a religion

- The psychological and dogmatic impact of a religion

- The rate of attraction or coercion and stress exerted by the religion.

- The use of technology, the impact of emotional pressure, advertising, media techniques, and other available resources that get people to join the religion.

This is the era of plurality of doctrines, a multiplicity of religions in a global society. It is politically correct to consider religion a mixture of eclectic beliefs, opinions, and philosophies that allow all religions to fit in. Everything is relative and suggestive. Nothing is absolute. The success of any congregation is measured according to the number of members, the real estate value, and the number of star personalities that belong. It is almost a must to come up with a doctrine that is flexible, and where everything is carefully prepared not to offend anyone. Because man is naturally inclined to believe in a supernatural being, some may take advantage of this innate search for the supernatural to teach pernicious doctrines. Since you are born with a strong desire to succeed, when you are oppressed it is only natural to believe it when they tell you that your current situation is God's will; it does not take a rocket scientist to make you want to repudiate such a belief. You cannot remain indifferent when members of your family, your ancestors, your friends, and your children have been abused in the name of religion.

Another extreme is to tell you that those who exploit you and yours represent the "great Satan," or that which needs to be eliminated in the name of the greater good, in order to have everlasting life in paradise. This also makes you wonder. Furthermore, if you are told that you can become a martyr, you will go straight to heaven, and your family will be taken care of; this is a serious offer that if you are naïve enough you may consider.

When you are denied even the bare minimum because of prejudice, discrimination, and abuse, religion will again determine your choices. You can become an easy target for subversive teachings. You may think about destroying others in this world to inherit a marvelous life in paradise. You may feel you have little time and discernment to realize that this is also a false doctrine, a misuse of religion for wicked and selfish advances. You need to realize that those who preach this kind of doctrine do not believe in it themselves; otherwise, they would have been the first people in line to kill themselves, but they are not. Others believe in these doctrines and follow them blindly, and the result is a polarized, poisoned world. It is a jungle where everyone is ready to defend himself by any means and at any cost. When religion becomes a means to get even for all supposed abuses sustained, it becomes dangerous and counterproductive. Hate begets hate. War and destruction begins a vicious cycle. When people can hide behind religion to make themselves immune from critique, to usurp supreme power, and push people to do all kinds of repugnant acts, the result is complete chaos. The whole world situation makes people even more confused.

Some people conclude that they have a choice between a "modern religion" and "self-made religion." In reality, there is one true religion, with several carbon copies. Pulled between a plurality of traditions, ancestral and cultural influences, and the multiplicity of current influences, the tendency is to adopt a syncretized and blurred religion. For the contemporary religion to be successful, it has to be popular, conformist, non-confrontational, and adorned with all the popular up-to-date customs. It has to be entertaining; thus, it is measured in relation to popular shows and programs like MTV. Truth becomes synonymous with personal preferences, viewpoints, and intuitions. Religions flirt with good and evil. They play between worldly pleasures and guidelines from the supernatural.

Religion is seen as a private matter where everyone does whatever is comfortable. Nothing is absolute and nothing is holy. Everything is questionable and must pass the Cartesian test. Even the hierarchy of values is put aside to embrace the freedom to create your own religion. Paradoxically, such an approach makes religion more popular but less substantial. It makes many hardcore conservatives worried, because the fundamentals, such as faith, hope, and love, are not quantifiable values; they are seen through the lifestyle of a believer.

You can fall in love with religion, yet not be engaged in it the right way or for the right reason. Nevertheless, if you seek success on all levels, there must be a set of criteria to make you successful with religion. You must identify the true religion! You need to familiarize yourself with a set of invariable truths that can distinguish true religions from all the imitations. If everyone everywhere believes that he is living in truth while having his own respective experiences, then truth loses its meaning. Truth cannot be suggestive; it cannot be the fruit of your capricious agenda. Among the monotheists, the polytheists, and the atheists, who really hold the truth, the whole truth, and nothing but the truth?

Let us consider the monotheist believers: What is the name of their God? Is it Jehovah, God, Yahweh, Allah…? How does He reveal himself to His believers? Is it through the Bible, the Koran, or some other means? If it is through the Bible, is it through the Talmud or the Torah? The Old Testament or the New Testament or both? Are there parts of the biblical writings that are apocryphal? Why? These are just a few questions raised by a network of multidirectional beliefs. These questions already place people in different camps. Everything depends on so many factors and circumstances. No one seems to be sure whether he is right or wrong.

In a civilized world, we should have a formula to find a healthy ground to get together, get along, and come up with an ecumenical consensus, to the point where prayers are addressed to the Almighty as a being, who can be either male or female, with no name and no clearly defined characteristics. The approach also must take into account the groups that do not accept this solution. The result becomes an amalgamation, a series of confusions, and an atmosphere of total chaos. Nevertheless, there must be a true religion! Let us remember our premise: If every religion in this world holds its own truth, then there is no difference between truth and lies. If all the beliefs lead toward the light, then light becomes darkness. If all the assemblies that claim to practice justice do indeed practice justice, how would we then define justice?

The first genuine step toward uncovering the true religion is to gather certain key facts: convictions, ethics, etiquette, and invariable moral values. This religion cannot accept ambivalence or the tendency to follow the crowd. True religion requires deep knowledge and the experience of what is learned through humility, dedication, altruism, and a total obedience to the Supreme Being. Can man be wholly perfect in the observance of the religious dogmas of his religion? The ultimate religion maintains a harmonious relation on both levels: horizontally vis-à-vis his neighbors and vertically towards the Supreme Being. It requires a dynamic faith and a sincere devotion, as well as a deeply rooted and progressive knowledge of the given doctrine.

You accept a system of supernatural beliefs that consciously or unconsciously guide you in your daily existence. Your conscience leads you to believe that some acts are reprehensible, while others are commendable. Your curious nature wants you to continue to search for truth. The challenges come when you have to decide how much truth you are willing to seek. After you find it, how much of it you are willing to obey and apply to your personal life?

You will discover quickly that truth tends to pull you away from the easy, selfish life and to lead you toward a life dedicated to pleasing a higher power. There lies a great conflict. If you really want to be at peace with your inner self, you should target the ultimate truth. It is not a mere choice between the good, the bad, and the less bad. The struggle should instead be between the truth and the lies, with the understanding that half-truths will not do. You must erect solid pillars of your authentic beliefs: faith, knowledge, and obedience. Religion is not the affair of a nation, group, or community; it is not a big umbrella under which everyone gathers in bad times for permanent security and salvation. The true religion requires personal action by everyone to uncover "the truth, the whole truth, and nothing but the truth." It is not inherited from parents; it is a personal, individual choice.

You cannot be a passive spectator. You must answer the pertinent question: Is there a God? And if so, who is He? Who is Jesus Christ? Is he just a historic figure? Or is He the Son of God? He said, "I am the way, the life and the Truth; no one comes to the father but by me" What did He mean by this? How could He make such a statement? Was He an impostor? Rest assured He couldn't be the Savior of this world and an impostor at the same time. What role does He play in everyone's life? If God is not the Creator, the ultimate Maker of the universe, somebody else and something else must be in control.

These pertinent questions make religion a matter that must concern all. It is not only for the theologians and the believers; it is everyone's business to take a stand. And this can only be done based on the knowledge and influences received. You should not wait until you die before you address these questions; by then, it will be too late. Why take any chances? You must have an idea about your becoming after death. And you had better err on the side of wisdom, rather than on the side of foolishness.

The majority of the people in the western world (for various reasons, including geographic location) believe in a transcendent God who made the universe and is the source of all beings on this planet. The Abrahamic monotheist reveals an omniscient, omnipresent, and omnipotent Yahweh. This belief in the uniqueness of God is shared by the Jews who are still waiting for the advent of the Messiah, the Christians who believe that Jesus Christ was the Messiah, and the followers of Islam who talk about a God (Allah) who never ceases to create; He owns and inherits all. There are also other beliefs: Buddhists acknowledge a duality between existence and suffering; life is defined as the dimension of pain. Among the followers of Confucius, the Chinese believe in a cyclic time and an everlasting continuity; they speak of man, the heavens, and earth. Gnostics, too, have their own faith, and the list goes on.

Religion is a hot topic, as well as a delicate and thorny concept. You cannot afford a wishy-washy approach to the subject, nor should you avoid broaching the subject for the sake of being politically correct. Let the chips fall where they may. Whenever you dare to talk about it, you are bound to step on a few toes and you may even commit a few blunders. The subject is worthy of your concern.

You are a product of your family, education, instruction, genetic composition, and the culture and society from which you evolved. Religion influences these factors. When someone says, "I am an atheist" (after careful consideration, I hope), such an exclamation does not distance him from religion. To the contrary, this is a statement about his spiritual beliefs. Show me any human being in action, and he will act based on his convictions, which are his life credos. Your religion determines your lifestyle and the way you accept life.

You find religion in economic policies, social, educational, cultural, familial, physical, intellectual, mental, material, legal, and moral institutions. Religion judges and influences marital status, procreation, abortion, education, professional choices, politics, science, and technology. History reveals facts about old rituals, traditions, ancestral practices, as well as faith, liturgy, and superstitions.

The words cult, religion, sect, life, immortality, and mortality do not necessarily have the same meaning for all. For instance, some show deference to rats, while others see rats as a pestilence to be destroyed. Some love to eat beef, and others die hungry while honoring the cow.

If you consider all the inhabitants on this planet, you find a conception of religion that forces you to think. On the one hand, there is a polytheistic approach, where animation and origin of life have a peculiar definition and understanding: soul, wind, fire, water, earth, space, inertia, equilibrium, and energy play a key part in the life continuum. On the other hand, there is the belief in a Supreme Being who created all, including man, who is superior to the rest of the earthly inhabitants. In between these two beliefs, there are various other beliefs that bring about so many different religious institutions. Throughout life, you must find your way, while being pulled in various directions. You must pick and choose between all available doctrines, including your natural, innate, carnal desires, and the sublimity of your faith. There is a constant struggle between man's corporeity and his spirituality, between the temporal and the eternal; this is not an easy task.

All these religions, with their disparate rhythms and practices, are confusing. When you analyze their doctrines, you find a paradoxical message: How can you have so many truths? Is it possible to have so many religions, while all claim to have the truth? If all of these churches, cults, and sects represent truth, there is therefore no such thing as a lie or mistake. However, you know that errors, lies, and mistakes exist in various domains. So is it possible for religion to be the exception? The answer is logically clear: No! Why? There are those who believe in God as the Almighty Creator, those who believe that things evolved from a big bang, and those who believe that you are your own god; all of these cannot be right. Where is the truth? Is it Confucianism, animism, shamanism, Totemism, Buddhism, Islam, deism, Taoism, theism, Christianity, postmodernism, pantheism, individualism, fetishism, mysticism, humanism, Brahmanism, Jainism, Judaism, or atheism? These beliefs and philosophies cannot all hold the truth.

Suppose that Christianity is the true religion. What happens to the Chinese, who were never exposed to Christianity? The Chinese child is normally going to adopt his parent's and his country's beliefs. This is where religion becomes crucial.

To practice a dogma blindly is dangerous. A blind faith can lead you down the path of disaster. Your faith must be based on knowledge. You must be able to question what you are presented and make your own personal choice about your faith. You came into this world alone and you must decide alone, based on all the available data, on your own faith. Your religion cannot and must not be based on what the majority accepts. You need to do your own homework; it would be great to have a universal religion where everybody believed the same things. But even then, many would accept out of fear, not out of free will. You are not a robot, and you are not a slave. You were created with the freedom to think and choose. You must go beyond the concept of collective salvation. Your salvation, your ultimate destiny, depends on your personal choices.

Money and Religion

Any religion that seeks to limit man's potential, abilities or affect his surroundings becomes at the very least questionable in its doctrines. But for a lot of congregations, religion is nothing more than a compilation of rules, precepts, laws, and principles, with the emphasis on what not to do. This clips man's wings and dampens his aspirations. These churches have a long list of don'ts. Some reduce religion to the point of limiting intellectual performance. Some preach that you must live a life of poverty and austerity in order to inherit heaven. Money becomes evil, and material success makes people wonder whether or not the wealthy can be true Christians. Those religious people, who believe this negative viewpoint on wealth and money, are heaven-bound; they believe that whatever happens is God's will. They are focused on the afterlife, and they forget they are still living in this world. Those who grow up in such churches either remain faithful, head bowed forever until their death, or they revolt. Many quit those churches and pursue their own ways and beliefs, but not without a heavy conscience. When you neglect earthly living to embrace only the life to come, you risk missing out on both lives. After all, the way you live your life now will determine your everlasting destination. Jesus said, "You have been faithful in little things; I will give you more responsibilities." So, where does that fatalistic, poverty-stricken religion come from? Nowhere in the Bible is mediocrity and resignation condoned. The Bible gives plenty of examples of faith champions who had a successful life: Abraham, Joseph, Moses, Job, David, Solomon, and more.

The Bible contains about two hundred verses that deal with money. Throughout Jesus' earthly life, He dedicated half His parables and teachings to treating questions that deal with money handling, wealth, and management. He and His disciples warn against the love of money that can lead to regrettable acts; they were all against waste, negligence, and avarice. According to Matthew 25, the parable of the talents reminds us of a few points:

- All of us—without exception—have talents.

- The number and the diversity of these talents are unique and vary with each of us.

- The reasons we have these talents are many, including serving and perfecting the community of which we are a part.

The way we use our time, skills, and talents will determine our success or our failure. The day is twenty-four hours long for all of us. It is how these hours are used that makes the difference. A well-balanced life requires that we use what we have in the most efficient way. Our current life is short, and our needs and desires are unlimited. Therefore, it is necessary to act according to a set of priorities and seek after the opportunities that may come our way. If we remain passive and do nothing, what would prevent the Lord from asking us to give account of our administration? Who would we blame then? We believe we have individual responsibilities, familial responsibilities, as well as our responsibilities in our communities. The text continues: "for unto everyone that hath shall be given, and he shall have abundance; but from him that hath not shall be taken away even that which he hath." So if you are a parasite, if you are not diligent, the Bible calls you: "thou wicked and slothful servant." Our Creator is against laziness, as He said: "Six days shalt thou labor"

A healthy religion believes in work, success, and progress. A true believer must be disciplined and well-balanced. The spiritual and the material are not mutually exclusive. The secular world does just the opposite. Everything is tuned toward materialism, at the expense of the spiritual. This is not the way it should be. God must come first. But we must not only develop the spiritual. The Master clearly states in His parables that we must do our best with what we have; then, based on our performance; we may have access to more. The only thing Jesus cursed was a sterile fig tree. For Him, you must grow and produce or die. The apostle John expressed the wish that we prosper in every domain. A well-balanced Christian leads by an example of excellence in all that he is doing. The believer who is broke, poor, a beggar, envious, or lazy represents a challenge to the name of God, who is known to be the powerful holder of all things. He never makes an appointment with failures.

Nevertheless, while we are growing, progressing, and prospering, we must watch out for our motives and the ideas behind our success. God calls for a universal altruism. An authentic believer must realize it is normal to dream about having a beautiful home, a luxurious car, distinguished clothing, about going on vacation and sending your children to a good school. It is not a sin to reach a point where you do what you really like, as long as you honor God and practice the moral values and ethical codes. No matter what the circumstances are—in good times as well as in bad—what really counts is the condition of our spiritual lives, our attitude toward God and toward our fellow man. It is not a sin to be rich. The sin begins when money owns you and takes the place of God. Hell is a place for the rich as well as for the poor who chose not to accept God's salvation. When you have money to take care of God's cause, it is such a thrill. What a joy to help the poor and the needy, to develop community programs for the young, the elderly, and the underserved. And to do that, you need money. The problem is not money;

it is the place you give it in your life. How frustrating it is to see all the things you could do for your people, but you do not have a penny to help. Give me a choice between being poor or rich to serve the cause, and I'll take the latter anytime. The former has created enough frustration and heartbreak: to be so powerless in the face of so much need and so many dire conditions.

When you analyze the lives of those true believers who have distinguished themselves, there is one common denominator: They seek the Lord, they seek the truth to the best of their ability, and they act progressively as their knowledge increases. You can say they are successful servants. Here are the steps they have taken:

1. Realize there is a Supreme Being.
2. Seek to know Him through a systematic study of His words, through a personal experience with Him.
3. Believe in Him (to be successful, one must believe in someone or something).
4. Identify His will and choose freely to obey Him.
5. Depend on Him and consult with Him.
6. Let Him guide them in everything.
7. Realize we are in this world as God's ambassadors to advance His kingdom and to serve others.

May we all choose to start taking inventory about our eternal destiny! May we make an intelligent and beneficial choice! May we effectively witness that choice!

I have one last comment about the increasing number of people who define religion as being whatever is comfortable and acceptable for anyone, in other words, those who define religion according to what each person believes it is, as the product of our feelings, our moods, our desires, and our imaginations. These people say all religions are the same and have the same priorities, that the acid test is to find a doctrine that is emotionally stimulating and intellectually passionate. Truth becomes suggestive and varies with time and circumstances. Is this your viewpoint about religion? Then would you be so kind to reconsider and think again? Your current response determines your ultimate destiny. So don't let your eternity hang only on a probability! The choice is yours. It is your call.

Youth and Success

Defining Adolescence

Adolescence is the part of your youth that begins after childhood and lasts until you are financially stable, able to enter into the job market and play your role in society. In the twenty-first century, adolescence has become longer and more determinant in a person's future. This period affects the remaining stages of life, including adulthood, third age, and old age. This time in your life is pivotal.

The Worries of Adolescence

The world is a complicated place. A lot of decisions made by adults can mortgage the future of youth—increased world deficit, environmental issues, nuclear armaments, wars, terrorism, famine, and climate change. Youth itself often faces its own challenges—quality of education, health, social integration, career, job, and family problems. In the recent past, adolescents grew up generally carefree and disengaged from the world's affairs. Now, however, if adults and youth do not get together to address these concerns, the world is bound to face more unrest, violence, and extremism.

Unscrupulous and cruel adults looking for easy prey to enroll in reprehensible acts often exploit marginalized young people. Even some who are well educated and have decent jobs can, because of their lack of maturity and judgment, fall prey and become convinced to endorse and commit atrocities. We need concerted global efforts to:

- Help stabilize the families, which represent the first context for youngsters, and close the gap between parents and the next generation.

- Strengthen academic programs.

- Reevaluate the qualifications and philosophies of those who are teaching our youth.

- Address violence, inequality, injustice, and poverty, both locally and globally.

- Develop a plan of action for those who finish school and those who for various reasons have not reached the standards for a competitive position in the world market.

The physical, physiological, and psychological transformations of adolescence usually begin around the twelfth or thirteenth birthday, although they can occur earlier, especially in the developed countries. As a young person, you see changes that occur within you and that are beyond your control. You begin to see and feel things that you did not feel before. You have the impression that no one understands you and you tend to be confused. You are under construction or restoration, yet you neither see the architect to give him your point of view nor see the engineer or contractor to show them the blueprints. You are dying to have your say in such an important matter, as it concerns you and affects you for the rest of your life.

Parents who have been through such a chaotic period hope that their boys will come out charming gentlemen, mature and ready to decisively face the challenges of life. Their girls are expected to wind up beautiful princesses, who are nice, kind, and ready to sail victoriously through life. But whatever the goals, you have the opportunity to make it, even when you must go through trial, error, temptations, fights, privations, doubts, and hesitations. The road may seem long and tiring. Sometimes parents will ask whether or not the younger generation has what it takes to make it. The challenges will come everywhere and in all domains. The key is to stay the course and pursue your objectives.

As an adolescent, your main concern is the self. The different changes that take place make you uncomfortable, anxious, or confused. You worry about your appearance, the depth of your voice, your height, skin, weight, the hormonal roller coaster, and peer pressure from your friends. You are often pulled by the different options and demands that are imposed on you, especially those from your parents. You must perform in school and fulfill your assigned domestic duties. You want to look your best, and nothing seems to really help. Your friends have their own exigencies. The number of unanswered questions seems to grow daily. Sometimes the line that separates the normal turbulence of adolescence from pathology is blurred. You may become sad and anxious or even get depressed. You may find yourself alone in a dark hall with no direction. You are apprehensive about your parents, who want to help but do not always have the right approach. You tend to trust your friends, who lack knowledge or experience. Maybe you're irritable, indecisive, lonely, and angry, with no energy and no motivation to do anything. Or maybe you have taken the path of rebellion, arrogance, and ingratitude. Maybe you know someone who has even turned to violence, sexual promiscuity, and illegal substance use and abuse. Some adolescents become addicted, restless, unhappy, and depressed, and may even attempt suicide. The unpredictability of life and a lack of clear moral values can contribute to more despair.

The rigors of urban life do not make it any easier. Curiously enough, there are some pressing issues that may devour you, and you may feel that everyone is too busy to lend a listening ear. With the advent of so much technology, the opportunity to deviate and become addicted to the wrong habits is limitless. There are various reasons—loneliness, illness, poor self esteem, emotional disturbance, sentimental break up, social pressures, high family standards, familial and generational conflicts, confusion about sexual orientation, lack of or absence of parental authority or guidance, despair, etc.—that may lead you, the adolescent, to feel so desperate that morbid ideas seem like your only alternative. The level of discomfort and the reaction to all of these challenges depends on the individual. It all depends on your capacity to absorb.

If there is no moral compass and there are no reliable resources, suicide may come up as the quickest and most convenient exit. After all, how much can a novice endure on his first time around? Young folks should not automatically feel guilty if such an idea passes through their minds. This is merely a warning to make you aware of your predicament and force you to do a little backpedaling, to slow the fast and crazy pace of life, take inventory, and find the right direction. The main question is what to do? The answer is simple: seek help quickly. Do not rely on past prowess. Take a deep breath—give yourself some time to catch up. Seek company, avoid remaining alone in an isolated place, find or call someone to talk to. Remember, the time spent in a dialogue with someone can be a window of opportunity to find help, either from that person or someone else. It lowers the risk to pass to a regrettable and irreparable act. Do not discount spirituality!

Those who—one way or the other—destroy their lives can never experience the relief they longed for when they committed their desperate act. After all, those who are dead know nothing that is happening. Remember, when you stay alive, you always have a chance to get out of a jam. Everything—no matter what it is—is a temporary situation. Everything is temporal, even your worst sufferings. Therefore, if you are a deep melancholic, if you love to be alone with all kinds of ideas bouncing up and down into your brain, if you feel as if you are useless, purposeless, and insignificant, if you have lost all interest in what happens in the world, cheer up! If you have a hard time making decisions or staying focused, if your academic performance is dropping, seek help and do it quickly. You owe it to yourself to be curious enough to see what life has in store for you. If you must consult with a professional, do it and do it fast. If people can see a doctor for asthma, diabetes, anemia, and pain, it should be the same for mental challenges.

Do not take it upon yourself to carry the world's burden on your shoulders. Let a professional declare you safe and sane. Based on what the professional advises, you will learn to develop techniques to cope with your dilemmas. You need to determine your comfort zone and realize at what level your tanks become inoperative. You must find a way to cope with difficulties and increase your rate of endurance. There is always a better approach to do things, including coping with the challenges of life. It is foolish to try to learn through only your own experience. Talk to the older generation. If they are honest and their memory works properly, most of them will admit to having difficult and turbulent teenage years.

The Joy of Adolescence

Being young is one of the greatest privileges in life. You are only young once. Think about it: this is the time to build up your future. The opportunities are countless. You have a tremendous number of choices. The future of the world is in your hands. The most important acts of your life are ahead of you, while your elders can only look backwards on their own lives. They look at a past they cannot change; as an adolescent, you are looking at a future with a blank page on which to write your own script. The sky is your limit. You have the ability to see things with brand new eyes, and the stamina to find your own way of doing things. All things are possible. You can look forward to completing your studies or pursuing more advanced studies. You have a role to play in your family and in society. You can make responsible choices and contributions. Consider the variety and richness of your choices: different careers, lifestyle, level of education, choice of a life partner, falling in love, traveling, playing. You have the unique opportunity to make the most of the choices that will determine the curve of your life.

As a child, you were protected against yourself and you were totally dependent upon your parents to do almost anything; your life was even attached to theirs. Now that you are an adolescent, you need to grow on your own. Of course, you can enjoy your freedom along with some responsibilities. This is the period where you can make provisions for all the things you are going to need in life. Being young is the time to contemplate all the possibilities available. It is the time to dream, excel, learn, and study. Above all, you have the option to use the experience and guidance of your elders to help you avoid making the same mistakes they made in their own youth.

Do you know how many adults would beg to have the chance to relive their adolescence? Adults have so many responsibilities. They see their past mistakes, and they are often stuck paying the price. To avoid such future regrets, learn to take responsibility for your actions while you are still an adolescent. Character, personality, discipline, and good habits are the key determinants for future success as a young man or young woman. Adolescence provides the time to get rid of many shortcomings and nurture the strength of character required to make it in real life. While dreaming and seeking fun, you also must bring solutions and innovative approaches to the many problems created by the older generation.

Adolescence And Relationships

Youth—parent relationship

Some parents remain stuck in their past and want to duplicate the old-fashioned treatment they used to receive as a youngster: "As long as you are under my roof, you do as you are told—or else." In the twenty-first century, things have changed; yet some adults still have a tough time adjusting to the new era. It is difficult for them to admit that their kids, who still live at home, now all of a sudden want to participate in major decisions, while still enjoying the privilege of being as irresponsible as they were a year or two before.

Parents generally dream of having a good-looking, healthy, intelligent, nice, and well-mannered child. After all, it probably seems like it was just yesterday when they gave birth to their adorable baby, who was completely dependent upon them for anything and everything. They remember the various trips to the emergency room or the doctor's office and the countless sleepless nights, filled with anxieties and worries over a fever, ear infection, teething, and other threats that caused concern. All of a sudden, that tiny, lovely baby has become a young lady or a young man who wants to be treated accordingly. Suddenly that new person shows weird tastes in music, hairstyle, clothes, career aspirations, and even the way they talk and walk. Everything is different and contrary to the parents' own tastes.

The hormonal changes and the cultural conditions that should facilitate the child's maturity seem to contribute to the transformation of the little angel into a rebellious devil. The parent begins to ask a few questions: What has happened to my child? Is he normal? Will she become psychotic, manic, or depressed? Is he using any forbidden substances? What is she watching on cable or the Internet? Is he yielding to the bad influences of friends? Parents realize that this is a difficult period for their child. Yet it is difficult to allow the teenager enough room to maneuver without inconvenience. Parents should continue to support the child with unconditional love while the adolescent tries to navigate through life. During this time, parents should not be a source of increased stress. Young men and women will usually overcome their newly acquired tastes without lasting consequences (although tattoo removal can be painful).

Some young folks may need a series of regular sessions with a therapist; another, smaller, group requires a longer period of professional intervention. Overall, the majority comes out with a more or less normal life. This is why it is paramount that parents do their best while the child is growing up, so that they won't have to blame themselves if the outcome is not what was expected.

Parents should teach their children solid values, ethics, financial responsibilities, etiquette, the sanctity of life, love, respect, discipline, diligence, integrity, patriotism, the sense of service to others, and spirituality. The parents' behavior and lifestyle is the best example for the children. All children and adolescents hate hypocrisy. The parents' key role is to be there and help the kid go through those various moments in his or her life. The parents must avoid being judgmental or antagonistic. The emphasis must be on the positive approach to life.

Many subjects will trigger clashes or misunderstandings between parent and child: household chores, the choice of friends, academic performance, career choice, and sexual behavior. This is an adjustment period where the child is testing the boundaries. Parents should make sure they have firm foundations and firm boundaries, without being impossible to deal with. The adolescents should not press their luck either. Fairness from both sides is the key. Parents tend to keep quiet when everything goes their way. They do not congratulate their children for good behavior. There is no positive reinforcement. The child never hears one word of approval or even disapproval until a mistake is made; then the sky falls in. Some parents just focus on the child's weakness and never mention strengths.

Adolescents love to hear congratulatory remarks; they love to be noticed, acknowledged, and rewarded.

Sabina is a bright young lady. All her life her family never had to ask her to do her homework. All her teachers are proud of her and congratulate her parents for having raised such a gifted and distinguished child. At least three times while in junior high school, Sabina told her parents of a new choice for her career. One afternoon during the last months of her high school classes, she burst into her dad's study and blurted out, "Dad, now I know for sure what my career is definitely absolutely going to be: I want to be a pastor!" Her dad continued to read his newspaper, so she repeated herself.

Her father—with his customary nonchalance, his glasses halfway down his nose—then began a long tirade about life: "My dear daughter, the bunnies are friendly and they are always around, but they are quick. If you go after all of them, you run the risk of not catching any of them."

Upset, Sabina replied, "What do bunnies have to do with my career?" She left and closed the door behind her. Thus began an evening of hell at Sabina's house.

Whose fault was it? Anyone's? Couldn't the dad have shown a bit more consideration and chosen another time to teach her about the importance of being focused? Asking an adolescent to be certain of his or her career is stretching it a bit. Why did the father react that way? What was going on with Sabina? Maybe she wanted her dad to pay more attention to her instead of his newspaper? Was her dad acting out of his own bias about women pastors? Did she do it to challenge him? Or was it to catch his attention? Did he want her to become a lawyer like him and take over his successful practice?

How many times does a miscommunication between parents and children trigger so much anger and animosity? Many adolescents have doubts about their parents' love at the same time that their parents are killing themselves for a better tomorrow for their children. Something is wrong. Parents must find time to communicate with their children. They must be able to take advantage of the rare opportunity that the child sometimes gives them for a constructive dialogue and desperately needed advice in a difficult situation. How can parents have time to help others and not enough for their own household? Unfortunately, most adults are very busy trying to prepare a better way for their children. But the best gift a parent can give is to be available to a child at any time and at any age. So many parents regret not having created a special time at a crucial moment for their children.

Johnny wants to spend the night at a friend's house. He is all excited.

When an adolescent wants to sleep over at someone else's home, it is not the end of the world. It is a friendly and innocent request. But for responsible parents, this innocent request raises key questions: Who is that friend? Who are the parents? Who else lives in that house? Are the parents going to be there or are they on a trip, leaving the house in the hands of a bunch of teenagers? Sometimes, the suspicion of the parents can be due to a memory of their own misdeeds or bad experiences. They want to make sure they do not make a decision that can short-circuit their child's life and even force him or her to take inappropriate and perilous detours in life. They want to protect their child. But at this age, the child feels invincible and immortal. The teenager believes that only the elderly can become seriously sick or die. Even when misfortune befalls one of their friends, the shock does not last for long.

Adults, however, know that everyone is vulnerable and bad things can happen to good people. Where parents see danger, the adolescent sees excitement. Many parents have had to learn this the hard way. They have had quite some bad experiences. Out of all of these hardships, they have earned enough wisdom and they are anxious to pass it on, to help the new generation avoid those pitfalls. Alas! A fool must learn from his own bad experiences, but the youngsters still insist on doing it their way. Each home has its set of rules and principles, its own way of conceiving things. The role of parents and, in general, the role of established authority is rather unpopular with most adolescents. They resist authority figures. Here is a melodrama that is being played, and the outcome depends on the performance of the actors. They must avoid being blind and deaf and shouting at each other, while driving at high speeds on a road full of curves, bumps, and cliffs on both sides.

Parents should slowly allow more and more independence to the adolescents and trust them a bit more. Adolescents should not have to doubt or second-guess their parents' motives, which are love and care. Remember, trust must be earned.

Relationship with friends

The best way to know and count your true friends is through hardships. For young folks, life is generally exciting, and people tend to share that excitement. It is socially healthy to be friendly and affable and to meet people. Nevertheless, you need to be careful as to the quantity and the quality of the friends you make. According to the Greek philosopher Aristotle, there are different types and different levels of friendship. Adolescence is a vital period in your life, and a genuine friendship can help you sail through life successfully. But a mischievous friendship can put you on the road to destruction and burial. To compensate for your lack of experience, as a well-tuned adolescent, you must set some criteria and some acid tests to determine who should be your friend and who should not be. The characteristics for a durable friendship include:

- The maturity to maintain a reciprocal friendship.

- Prioritizing each other's interests and well-being.

- Actively listening to each other, forgiving each other, and receiving constructive criticism from each other.

- Being there for each other in times of trouble.

The false friendship is selfish, superficial, jealous, hypocritical, one-sided, and deviant. The authentic friendship is rare, but it survives the wear and tear of life.

Bear in mind these keys:

- Life is made up of choices, and each choice has its consequences. Be careful before making any choice, because the price may be too high.

- Being young does not make you immortal or invincible. You must learn to diminish risk, stay out of trouble, avoid dangerous activities and places, and avoid going beyond the limit of your bravado.

- The world contains evil, including drugs; violence; sexual, physical, and emotional abuse; sexually transmitted diseases that can change and shorten your life; suicide; and various noxious things that compete for your thoughts, choices, and attention.

- You become what you think and act upon. And what you think stems from what you see, read, and hear; the places you go; and the people with whom you interact.

The biggest challenge is to have enough maturity and self-confidence to know what you want. Do not yield to peer pressure that pushes you to act inappropriately and do things you know are not right. Many of the activities you are asked to participate in will appear benign. They may seem exciting and full of fun initially, but in reality they are foolishness with regrettable consequences. For example, so-called friends may tell you it is fun to steal from a store, steal a car, go for a joy ride, flirt with people passing by, or hitchhike down the road. They may tell you it is cool to smoke and take drugs. They may make fun of you if you are strict and disciplined. They may call you names, or find you too rigid and boring. They will tell you it is macho to have a gun, to fight with gangs, etc. Some may even require that you commit some specific act to be admitted in their gang or club. They may use various approaches to get you involved in illegal and illicit acts. If they succeed, you may find that the rest disappear and leave you, the new initiate, standing at the scene of the crime. You must be prepared to stand your ground in the first place and not go along, but go your own way.

Once you take the first wrong turn, it is often a downward slippery slope that brings pain, suffering, remorse, and damnation to yourself and all of those who really love and care for you. Do not fall into the trap of peer pressure to do evil. Beware of those who speak too loud and brag about performing various misdeeds. They may actually not be the doer but the pusher who gets others in trouble.

I still remember a few of my high school friends who always had condoms in their pockets. They constantly bragged about their multiple performances. It turned out most of them were bluffing, and the girls they were talking about were just in their fertile imaginations. At any rate, be it true or false, you have no place for foolishness.

- Parents generally wish the best for their children. They have experience and the wisdom. Ask for their guidance, and you will double your own wisdom and knowledge.

Peer pressure

Adolescents hear the term peer pressure more than any other age group. But peer pressure is always there at any stage in life. The key difference is that youth are more vulnerable to peer pressure, because the young person is at a crucial corner when he can make the wrong turn for lack of the proper guidance and support. Adolescents do not really trust their parents. The young person is closer to those who belong to the same age group. Unfortunately, they do not have the experience. They rely on what they read, what they see, and what they watch on television. Their idols can be celebrities they've never met or even seen in real life. How many young people get drunk and become drug addicts through their own initiatives? Not many. More often, it starts with a friend who looks "cool," "happy", "friendly," and "caring." The irony is that this so-called friend may never cross the limit, while the one introduced to those bad habits may become hooked for life and ruined forever.

Love

When you are young and blossoming like a beautiful flower in the springtime, obviously you are noticeable and attractive. The hormonal changes you are going through also give you some hints. At this stage of the game, boys meet girls, girls meet boys, and they notice each other. Two people meet each other, talk, exchange ideas, and discuss mutual interests.

The Internet provides many opportunities to meet people you would not otherwise have the opportunity to meet. There are many safe ways to look for individuals whose profiles are similar to your own, in terms of views and interests. However, because the Internet also makes it possible for people to disguise their true identity, you need to exercise appropriate caution.

Follow the basic safety rules for contacting people you meet online, but as an adolescent you should follow some extra rules, too. The reason is that young people are particularly attractive targets for predators, and, because of your limited experience in the ways of the world, you may also be more easily taken in than an experienced adult would.

- When you put your own profile on a dating or social networking site, do not reveal identifying information, such as your address or phone number. Use an email address that does not lead directly to your family's home.

- Use only sites that are designed for young people and have safety features in place specifically to protect young people from predators, but don't rely on those features for your full protection.

- Do not visit or associate yourself with a site that permits links to pornographic or other so-called adult material.

- If you meet someone online, whom you are interested in meeting in person, review the person's profile with your parents, being completely open with them about your interest in meeting this person.

- The first time you meet such a person in real life, do not go alone or with your friend. Go with one of your parents and tell the person you will be doing this. Arrange to meet in a public place, such as a coffee shop or a bookstore or library. Do not reveal your address or phone number in advance of the meeting.

- Trust your parents' judgment in these matters. They have your best interest at heart. They have known you all your life.

- Before you go out alone with the new person, go out a few times with a group of friends to engage in a social activity such as team sports, bowling, skating, or eating as a group at a restaurant.

When you are getting ready to go out with someone, follow these guidelines.

Young women

- Wear decent clothes to avoid giving the wrong message and be aware of what you are saying with your body language. A tight dress, skirt, or pants, or a very short skirt, and showing off your chest give a much louder message then a verbal "No".

- Avoid any partner who shows signs of being abusive, obnoxious, intoxicated, rude, vulgar, obscene, or disrespectful.

- Watch for signs that may lead to unwanted advances: the consumption of alcohol and/or drugs; attempts to touch aggressively; pressure to go out alone and be in abandoned, dark areas, or isolated halls with very loud music; or invitations to sexually explicit, pornographic, or violent movies. These are big signs of impending danger. Stop before it is too late.

- Beware of the standard pressure phrases that seemingly emerge anew in the mind of every hormone-charged young man: "Come on, baby! You know I love you," or "Don't be ridiculous, everybody is doing it," or "Don't be so uptight and boring," or "If you only knew the pleasures you are missing." Be in charge of your own body; know yourself.

- When you are going to go out with someone you don't know well, there is always the chance of arguments and confrontations. If that partner insists on making you do or take steps after you firmly say, "No!" you must be willing and able to fight and survive: Yell with all the strength of your body, your lungs, and your vocal cords.

- If he tries to physically force you do something that you don't want, locate the most sensitive and vulnerable parts of his body and shock him with the best kick of your life. Then run for cover with all your strength, once you deem it safe to do so. Use your common sense to always come out alive.

- Some people carry a can of pepper spray (in places where it is legal to do so), a loud whistle, or an air horn. The main thing is to avoid dangerous situations in the first place.

Young men

- Try to know as much as you can about the other person.

- Do not put yourself in a situation where you have no choice but to do something you did not intend to do.

- Do not go on a date with someone just because of what your friends told you about her.

- Respect yourself and your date, and avoid compromising situations.

Both

Rather than seeking a casual romantic encounter, look in your community, your church, your social gatherings, your school, or your university to find someone who is decent enough to share some cordial relations, dialogue, or lunch. There is nothing shameful in girls or boys having attractions and sexual feelings. The important thing is to control the impact of sex on other higher priorities at this stage in your life, such as your studies.

When you find someone with whom to have a relationship, what is next? Do you spend all your time talking, sharing emotions, apprehensions, plans, dreams, and fears for the future? Or instead, do you plunge head over heels into all sorts of intimate activities. In love, the more we eat, the hungrier we may become.

Adolescence is a time when unexpected things can happen, and you tend to overestimate your strength. Many discover too late that there is a point of no return. When you play with fire, you may get burned. Do not let yourself be consumed by the incandescent passions of love. There is risk in forcing events prematurely and becoming more vulnerable than you initially conceived.

Sex

As a young person, you seek the freedom to stand on your own and do what you want. But real freedom is not the right to do what you please, as you please, whenever you please, and with whom you please. It is instead the ability to do what you are required to do, what you are expected to do, and what you ought to do, and do it gracefully, without complaining or murmuring. It underscores the idea of choice. The main prerequisite for all choices includes knowledge, maturity, and the ability to face, deal with, and live with the results of your choices. You are never free enough to do away with the consequences of your choices. You are never free enough not to submit to the impact of the choices you make. Life is unfair because often you do not get what you think you deserve. Unfortunately, the bad consequences never fail to haunt you. We are all subject to the choices we willfully make. Only you should be blamed for what you choose to do. Anyone who engages in intimate relationships with a partner must make sure they know what they are getting into and be prepared to face the consequences of such a choice. The impact of such an act is often long-lasting and may completely torpedo your future. One night of pleasure can ruin the entire life of someone, by forcing upon you all kinds of unforeseen woes that could have been avoided. The only sure thing is that if you abstain from engaging in sexual acts before you are really ready to do so, you cannot get pregnant and do not have to worry about all the headaches shared by those who chose to do otherwise. Remember, you have your entire life to enjoy an intimate relationship with the person of your free choice. What is the rush? Are your peers or the current culture pressuring you? If you get in trouble, remember you will be on your own. When you are ready and when you decide by your own free will to engage in such activities, make sure it is a well thought out and wise decision that is taken for the fulfillment of a loving relationship. You are not a piece of meat at the mercy of a buyer, who wants to touch, feel, and taste you before buying. You are a special being who came into this world at a special moment for a special purpose. You did not come into this world just by pure hazard or luck. You must not sell yourself short. You must affirm yourself and take your spot under the sun.

As you prepare yourself for a definite commitment, engage in several activities that can help you develop your faculties. Activities such as sports, family occasions, and community services will enhance your self-worth. Make full use of your various talents and abilities. Feed your mind with noble ideas; read excellent books; be careful about who your friends are, what you read, what you hear, what you listen to, and what you watch. You are pulled in various directions, but you must use caution and discernment, cultivate good ideas and excellent habits, and gravitate toward the people who can lift you up and not bring you down. While cruising on the highway to success, a bump or a pothole can wreck you and put you completely out of the circulation for yourself and your family. So beware! Be vigilant; be courageous, bold, and steadfast; and do not cave in to the pressure to join the crowd. Be at peace with your enlightened conscience. You will never regret it.

One mistake can mark you for life and make you lose or become unable to enjoy the results of your most precious gifts, talents, and wealth.

A beautiful young lady is in high school. She is full of hope, energy, and special goals. Eventually she falls in love with a young man, and her parents get wind of the situation. They speak to her and show her all the reasons to stay focused on her studies, get good grades, obtain a scholarship, and gain admission to a good college for a bright future. But she is in

PRESCRIPTION FOR A SUCCESSFUL LIFE

love and she believes this is really it. She does not want to live without this specific guy. The two continue with their relationship. They find all kinds of excuses to meet and enjoy each other's company. One day their passion is so high it gets the best of them. They go all the way, and, although it feels good, six weeks later the young lady finds out she is pregnant.

What can be done? What is going to happen? Here are a few issues that automatically come into play:

- Both, or at least the young lady, will experience anxiety, fear, worries, regrets, guilt, and stress.

- What choice does she have: should she have a clandestine abortion, without even informing the guy who got her into so much trouble?

- What about her parents? She was forewarned before this happened. Now what role do the parents have to play? What are the parents' moral values, religious associations, and position?

- Should she contact the doctor alone, or with the parents, the boyfriend, or all of them?

- What if her decision is against the views of her boyfriend, parents, or both?

- Is abortion at her age forbidden or not? Does it require the parents' involvement, consent, or not?

- Are the people in that community conservative, liberal, pro-abortion, or against abortion?

- What are the religious, political, and psychological impacts of an abortion on her life?

- What about the fetus: is it a human being? When does he become viable and need to be protected by law against any attempt to kill him?

- Does the fetus have any rights? If so, who is going to fight for these rights?

- What about the community where the young lady lives: should they know or not, and if so, what will be their reaction?

- If the young lady decides to keep the baby, what would be the impact on her life, her boyfriend's life, and her parents' lives?

- What about the option of adoption?

Here is one little moment of uncontrolled passion shared by two innocent adolescents that triggers a domino effect that will affect many lives. You must not take the economic, social, and psychological impact of such a situation lightly. Especially the last: culpability, trauma, stress, the possibility of abortion, feelings of betrayal, loss of confidence, deception, and apprehension. The social, economic, intellectual, and moral repercussions must not be underestimated either. After an abortion, many women feel guilty for the rest of their lives. Could you imagine if, after such an abortion, the young lady goes on with her life, gets married later on, but unfortunately can never have another child? She will have a lot of personal questions to ask. If she goes ahead and has the child, she will still have some other questions unanswered, especially the impact on her strict parents, society, her education, her career, and her financial future. If the child turns out to show some unexpected weakness of character or some behavioral concerns, the mother may still wonder why, even though the outcome may not necessarily have any direct connection with the condition in which she became pregnant.

In summary, when facing any challenges, you must always think about the consequences. Adolescents, generally, tend to minimize the impact of some spontaneous actions and some may even ignore the danger that is looming and waiting for them. The first step is to consider the various options, then proceed by process of elimination, by weighing each choice and then taking the well-thought-out decision. Whatever the final selection is, there will always be personal, familial, religious, financial, legal, and socio-cultural repercussions. In the adolescent phase of life, you are bombarded with all kinds of information, advice, pressures, and demands. But it is necessary to have some parametric guidelines, so that one knows in many instances whether or not one idea or view is worth considering. Then from the remaining pool, you must take the time to analyze the options, make an educated synthesis, and decide which road to take. From every decision stems consequences that will set the course and mark your life for a very long time.

Get into the habit of training yourself into making valuable choices. The combination of all the choices is likely to determine the life you are to live. Each choice is a reflection of your judgment, tastes, education, beliefs, knowledge, and ethnic and cultural background, moral values, ethics, legal, financial, and religious standing. No choice is insignificant or inconsequential. These are little streams that feed the great rivers. Youth is the ideal moment to build character and personality. It is the time to make important choices, such as career or profession, companionship, sexual orientation, where to live, financial goals, and the kind of lifestyle desired. If you are wise enough and or savvy enough to exploit the experiences of your elders and benefit from their advice, your choices are likely to be well thought out and geared toward the ultimate goals in your life. The biggest handicap for many youth is the tendency to ignore or neglect the advice of adults and belittle its impact on their future.

You arrive at one of your favorite restaurants. They show you the menu and you choose the meal that seems to be the most delicious. They give you a list of all the ingredients that make it so delicious and make you salivate. You know you are allergic to one of the ingredients, and if you eat it you will develop swelling of the throat, tongue, and mouth, along with diarrhea and severe abdominal pain. The last and only time you ate this particular ingredient, you almost died in a hospital.

Would you still insist on eating that special dish at any cost, just to satisfy your appetite? Obviously, you know the reasonable answer is no.

You will often hear adults tell you the consequences of their foolishness. So why go through it yourself? Many people tried one cigarette for fun, got hooked for life, and died because of smoking. Many adults were once full of life, with bright futures and a lot of potential, tried some drugs just to please their friends, and became drug addicts, a waste for society, and a burden for their loved ones. It is time to wise up and make the most out of adult wisdom and past experiences. By so doing you can avoid their pitfalls and move on more steadily, faster, and with more confidence. Why reject the advice of people who have known you all their life, in order to follow your peers, who are at least as inexperienced as you are? When two blind men are walking together and encounter a hole, they will fall into it together.

The biggest challenge for adolescents is to know how to make the right choice, how to set priorities. But you are exposed to so many alternatives that you will tend to focus on a narrow selection, based on your limited experience. You tend to withdraw into your own self-made world instead of broadening your horizons and making a well-informed final decision.

The Internet and other recent technological advances have multiplied choices exponentially. There was a time when the world available to you was small and you had the option to explore everything, listen to it all, smell it all, taste it all, question it all, and then make an educated choice. Nowadays, people pre-select. You are no longer forcibly exposed to things you might not like initially but may learn to like later on. Now, whatever you reject a priori you might never encounter a second or third time. For example, in the past if you wanted to listen to a specific singer, you turned on the radio and heard a few others until your favorite came on. That gave you the chance to be exposed to other artists, other styles and nuances of music. It sharpened your judgment and your ability to appreciate a variety of music. You might have surprised yourself by discovering that you liked another type of music that you initially thought you wouldn't like.

Today, you can choose exactly and uniquely what you want to listen to. When you fill your iPod with thousands of examples of a specific kind of music, you are less likely to be exposed to other types of music. You have a self-inflicted limitation in choices, which also feeds your tunnel vision and your self-imposed limited mind-set. How do you know that your selection is the right one when you never have a chance to at least be exposed to other types of music?

Can you imagine someone who is so thrilled once he finds out that he can use a kerosene lamp or a candle as a source of light that he rejects any attempt to see the real electric light? When you isolate yourself in your cocoon, declaring "this is it," you leave no room for further improvement and success. The more you willingly diminish your exposure to different alternatives, tastes, styles, philosophies, and approaches, the less latitude you have to discern what is best to satisfy your needs. It is not wise to build your own secure wall around your comfort zone, to be exposed exclusively to what you believe are your only needs. By so doing, you will anesthetize yourself, slowly killing your innate curiosity to explore everything that is available. The best approach is to have some core values, ethics and knowledge to make wise choices regardless of the environment and the circumstances. You must not destroy your ability to select among many. Otherwise, your critical and analytical senses atrophy, your tastes become insipid, your sense of appreciation becomes dull and prejudiced. You become complacent and filled with a false sense of self-sufficiency. You reach a plateau and you are stuck.

Ten ways to be the young person most sought after

1. Do your best to know yourself, love yourself, and challenge yourself.

2. Be disciplined and responsible: see to it that whatever task you begin is finished to the best of your ability.

3. Strive to be the best at whatever you are doing.

4. Do not neglect the little things. Be helpful and considerate at home, clean up your room, and find a place for everything.

5. Be diligent and patient.

6. Stay away from bad company, bad crowds, and bad friends. Do not overestimate your strength and your ability to stay out of trouble. When you are in the company of troublemakers, you are already in trouble. Should anything wrong happen while you are with bad company, you will be a part of it and may even be the one paying the stiffest penalty, even though you may be innocent.

7. Do not go around breaking others' hearts. Be a dignified young person who can distinguish true love from lust and carnal desires.

8. Sexual acts underscore responsibilities, commitments, maturity, and risks. Engage in it only when you are ready.

9. Remember that the best way to distinguish yourself is to show discernment and wisdom.

10. Beware of the existence of evil. The devil can disguise himself as an angel of light.

How to be the ideal young lady

1. Know yourself and your abilities, believe in yourself and love yourself.

2. Do not let yourself be intimidated by your environment. Be true to yourself and develop self-reliance.

3. Beware of the wolves in sheep's clothing who want to take advantage of you.

4. Cultivate good manners and stay away from vulgarity, gossip, and bad habits, such as drinking, smoking, and taking drugs.

5. Master your impulses and control your temper.

6. Be cheerful, elegant, and beautiful, without being an eccentric.

7. Be a lady: a well-mannered distinguished person who imposes respect and civility.

8. Be altruistic and empathic.

9. Master the ability to adapt and see the other side of every issue (be open-minded, but well-balanced enough to know right from wrong).

10. Learn to respect and appreciate others.

Dear adolescents,

Remember that your parents dream of children who can make them proud: nice, gentle, studious, obedient, knowledgeable children, with good hygiene and refined tastes, who stay away from vices and bad company. Nothing hurts a parent more than to see his or her own child engage in a pathway that the parent knows, by experience and knowledge, will end in disaster. It is worst than a cancer that is eating him alive, it is worse than watching his own child about to be struck by a truck without being able to help. When your turn comes to be a parent, may be you will understand a bit what your mother, your father went through. Then, unfortunately, it may be too late to mend such a broken heart. Why wait? Please, remember your parents love you and their only vested interest is to see you blossoming and becoming fully successful in every step of the way. Alas! Parents do not always convey such a love in a way that is clearly understood and appreciated by their children.

Dear parents,

Your adolescents want you to trust them, respect them, and treat them like grown-ups. They do not like to be embarrassed in public by derogatory remarks about their walk, their hairstyle, their clothes, or their unsatisfactory performance in school or at home. They are always longing for your words of encouragement, private one-on-one dialogue, your advice, your hugs, and the repeated assurance that you love them unconditionally.

This materialistic world defines success according to one's possessions, acquisition, conquests, popularity, beauty, power, and social-climbing skills. The reality check leads us all to define success as the ability to develop oneself to a level where goals and ideals are pursued, priorities are well placed, and there is ascending mobility in every domain, with the strong desire to continue to excel and do better yet. Authentic success allows one to judge, think, search, and choose deliberately what one wants in life, without any fear of being degraded or driven up against a system, a person, or an oligarchy. Those who succeed realize success is not an exclusive gift or a unique talent detained by some supernatural force, to be passed upon to some exclusive people at the expense of all the others. Success is governed by the choices and actions that we take daily. If you really care about succeeding in life, learn early and quickly how to navigate safely in this tormented world until you can reach the shore safely. Learn to take the appropriate steps and make yourself available to take advantage of any opportunities that pass your way. After all is said and done, if anyone has a great opportunity to succeed, it is the youth.

Women and Success

A Woman's Role Throughout the Centuries

A dream usually comes from an idea, a wish, a desire, a need, or a void that one seeks to fill. It starts as a vague, simple idea that takes form and shape to either become an illusion, quickly put aside in the big drawers of shattered dreams and disappointment, or an obsession that does not want to go away until it is explored, reviewed, cherished, acted upon, and made into a reality. Just thinking about it gives you energy, confidence, strength, and a sense of being on top of the world. For a dream to become a reality, you must be willing to travel a road with a lot of potholes, bumps, and curves; or you must jump off a plane without a parachute. It requires the willingness to try anything and everything, to risk all, to be ready to meet all challenges head-on, and never rest until your dream comes true. A dream you pursue casually or timidly is not going to happen. You need total commitment and full engagement. Any hesitation may make you unfit to pursue it. Any yield to discouragement may make you stop prematurely. The postmodern world we live in has had to face several key challenges. One of them, which requires your consideration, is the role and condition of women.

During antiquity, the Western world had a patriarchal approach to life. Men dominated in every domain; they made decisions and ruled according to their liking. For a long time, the woman's role was summarized as: giving birth, cooking, cleaning, sewing, taking care of every one else's needs, and keeping their mouths shut. Under the universal masculine domination, women were always in the background, to be seen but not heard from. Women were stereotyped as immature, of lower intelligence than men, and lacking in judgment. They were the victims of various kinds of abuse.

Throughout written history, from Plato to Freud and beyond, many philosophers induced from the biological differences between the sexes all kinds of strange theories; they advocated and rationalized all kinds of inequalities between men and women. During the Middle Ages, some even questioned whether women had a soul. They treated them as slaves or domestic animals. Others went so far as to deny women the rights of citizenship. But a man's success depended mostly—if not solely—upon the faithfulness and support of a woman. Her pivotal role was discrete but always important. She did everything behind the curtain for the public radiance of her husband and the success of her children, only to be repaid with arrogance, selfishness, and presumptuous remarks from men, including her husband and sons. Yet throughout all the ages, most great men were reared by, prepared by, and guided by a dynamic woman.

The woman found pride and personal accomplishment in the success of her husband and her children and in the expansion of their domain. She participated in the domestic administration of the family enterprises, and she was deeply involved and dedicated to the children's education and instruction. Her husband was to be well-liked, well-groomed, well-fed, and well taken care of, because anything her husband or child did was seen as a direct projection of her. The appearance and the image projected by the family through the husband

and children was a vote of confidence or rejection for the spouse. In that crucial, merciless role, to prepare all children to become great citizens for society and to assure the stability of the home, she was often neglected or pushed in a corner as a second-class citizen, whose life revolved around her husband and children.

The woman was sometimes the victim of abuse and cruelty of all kinds. She used to invest all she was and all she had in the home. But then if she was injured or ill or was abandoned or widowed, there were in many societies no provisions for her protection or support. When the children left home to set out on their own, the husband either continued to work or became interested in other activities or other, younger women. The poor wife became a negligible entity, dropped in a corner and treated according to the capricious choices of the almighty husband. She was forced to reminisce about her old days and share the ice cold company of an imposed silence. Often, life was unbearable for her. There were instances when she hoped to die in order to go to heaven, as her only escape for a better life. She had nothing, no financial independence. Everything rotated around the husband, who was the sole provider and the sole beneficiary of all the goods and services, while the wife shared all the burdens. The poor spouse became the object of all kinds of mistreatments or even blackmail. Curiously enough, in spite of mistreatment, the woman had always shown love, admiration, patience, and understanding.

Then patiently, slowly but surely, she began to make a few steps in the community where she had always lived. First in the neighborhood, she began to share and promote vital ideas that had been very useful for the success of the community as a whole. As she presented the various viewpoints to improve her quality of life at home and in the neighborhood, people started to listen to her, to analyze her opinions, which contributed to the betterment of the society. The horizons widened and brightened, and the interventions became more significant. Along came various scientific and technological advances in various domains that had also contributed in helping to clear the way for women. The economic, financial, scientific, and technological changes played their part on the road toward female emancipation and liberation. Where the light of knowledge penetrated, the darkness of ignorance must cease and desist. The fight was against resistance to change, prejudice and fears, for control of her body, financial autonomy, and access to education. These are a few of the contributing factors that have had a great impact on society in general, and particularly on women.

As families, schools, communities, various organizations, establishments, systems, and nations stopped demeaning women's capabilities and started to appreciate their invaluable contributions to the society, the imaginary fence between man and woman slowly dropped. Children of both sexes started having the same opportunities in all domains.

In this twenty-first century, no one in his right mind can doubt the contribution of women in the different sectors of society. She has been in the midst of the socio-cultural evolutions of the twentieth century. The actual trend leads her to be able to deal with many challenges, including aging gracefully without having to feel dependent upon anyone else, taking advantage of every phase of her existence, and making the most out of her own life for herself.

Women's condition has appreciably improved compared to centuries ago. Women are steadily making their way in the workplace, in many fields, such as business; education; psychology; behavioral, health, and social sciences; computer science; mathematics; and many more. Women hold key positions in large firms and are doing well as entrepreneurs in various industries. Nevertheless, they still have a long way to go in a world still dominated and ruled by men.

The rules of the game have increased the woman's load without the proper rewards. People expect the woman, on the one hand, to be the perfect wife and the gracious queen of an impeccable home. She must see to it that she is an irreproachable mother who raises perfect kids and an irreplaceable wife who keeps a well-balanced home. She must continue to charm and captivate all the attention of her husband and fulfill his needs, even when he reveals himself to be immature and insecure. On the other hand, she is also expected to pursue a career and a profession of her choice in a world where different forms of discrimination—spoken or unspoken—swarm. She also must perform extremely well in her working environment to prove herself. And if anything goes wrong either at home or at work, she is blamed even for things that are far beyond her control.

The woman's success is therefore defined as the sum of her performances, both at home and at work. The main dilemma is to find a formula whereby a woman can be accepted and classified as a success in the twenty-first century. In other words, in this postmodern era, what main criteria can be used to declare that this woman has been successful or not?

The principles for success must be uniform and should not necessarily vary according to your sex. The seed of success is budding within every soul. Everyone has dreams. The key difference is what you do with these dreams. Throughout the years, those dreams must find ways to blossom, be cultivated, grow, mature, and bear fruit. Otherwise, they are dead and must be thrown out in the garbage. The results depend on your choices, your plan of action, and the steps you take to make those dreams come true. Your choices depend on your formation, your character, your values, your beliefs, your connections, and your habits. Each time you opt to do one thing, you automatically renounce doing another thing.

Because your resources are limited, you must make the best choices and allocate your resources wisely for the maximum amount of return; time is of the essence. You cannot go back and verify whether or not the other option would have been better or worse. For example, when you choose to be a doctor instead of a lawyer, you have no opportunity to verify whether or not you could have been better off by being a lawyer. This detail is to stress the fact that you do not have time to keep going back and forth by trial and error. Whatever you choose to do, you must be dedicated to making it work and completely committed to succeeding with your choice.

When you evolve from a home, a community, a school system, a town, a city, a society, a nation, or a world where the mirror of common sense is broken or the compass of equity and fairness disappears, where everything seems to be turning around the best spinning skills; or when the customs, routines, and old-fashioned erroneous beliefs persist, you must be willing to fight against the waves of ignorance in order to shine the light of truth. The truth is that women and men are different in many ways, but they are not inferior or superior to each other. You need to stay focused and not be distracted by declarations and deeds that go contrary to the real truth.

Challenges Faced

As a general rule, people can talk about, write about, and dream of success, but the only way to make it is through hard work and perseverance. It is no exception for a woman. Nevertheless, a woman has some specific obstacles to overcome in order to make it.

History

History has not been favorable to women. Western civilization has inherited many beliefs, traditions and customs from the Judeo-Christian and Greco-Roman eras. Although rich and indispensable to our current culture, such a heritage has influenced us in ways that become as natural as a knee-jerk reflex. For many centuries, women's rights and privileges were ignored. In the Greek world, women and men had different and separate lives. The feminine life was purely a private matter. The "race" of women were known by epithets, such as people who practice deceit, violence, jealousy, lies, vanity, fragility, and coquettishness. Because women were for peace and against war, abuse, and aggression, many playwrights accused women of being against the established system.

Women's freedom and the relaxation of manners were alleged to have contributed to the downfall of the Roman Empire. In the past, among the appreciable and positively acknowledged contributions made by women was the development of Christianity, to which women contributed both materially and spiritually. In spite of the misogynist social norm, in the twelfth century women came to be seen as objects of romantic desire. What arose was the culture of the courteous knight *(le chevalier courtois)*.

From the Renaissance to the French Revolution, women had some role in politics and cultural events. Their personalities and feminine assets influenced the men on the throne. Through their literary works, which were appreciated in the salons, people had to talk about women, and they were allowed to be heard. However, as far as the general population was concerned, not much changed. Even the tentative appreciation in high places faced serious opposition and serious discussions. A look at the writings of such people as Molière, La Bruyère, Fénelon, and Marivaux will provide irrefutable proof of men's opposition to women's emancipation.

In the eighteenth century, the controversy took on another dimension. The most agitating question was whether women were inferior to men by nature or by education. (Bear in mind that men were ruling the world and were passing laws, including those forbidding or limiting woman's education.) The viewpoints became as polarized as the idea of "pro-life" versus "pro-choice" in the twenty-first century. Many were confusing anatomical differences with weakness. Some went as far as to declare physical weakness equivalent to intellectual weakness. The French Revolution did not change much in that regard. Napoléon Bonaparte's civil code put women under the guardianship of their fathers or husbands. Napoléon Bonaparte took away women's civil rights. When democracy arrived and the slogan *"Liberté, égalité, fraternité"* was devised, shouldn't it have addressed the

problem of inequality between men and women?
When Christianity proclaimed that everyone had a soul
that needed to be saved, what about the woman's soul?

Some men question a woman's right to work, while
in reality she has always been working. Since the
beginning of time, woman has never been idle. Her
tasks have included housekeeping, becoming pregnant,
giving birth, educating and raising the children,
cooking, cleaning, and sewing, supervising the servants'
performance, entertaining guests, and helping the
husband with the cattle and flock during the harvest
time. When she began to work outside of the house,
unfairness and exploitation became the norm.

When the industrialization of the world came about,
with all the prowess and progress in countless domains,
along with changes in life expectancy and cost of living,
and the social revolution in the second part of the
twentieth century, more and more women got involved
in the work force. But discrimination did not fade away.
Despite equal or better qualifications, the best jobs, the
best pay, and the promotions were still going to the men
of various companies. The debates have been going on
through the nineteenth and twentieth centuries, without
great results. But even if things are not where we expect
them to be, we must still admit that progress has been
made. The twenty-first century must really make the
difference. Women must continue to press on, become
more visible, better qualified, and run for political
and legislative offices, where they can really make a
difference through passion, pragmatism, commitment,
and their love for transparency and accountability.

Family and societal stereotype

Customs and traditions tend to perpetuate. Nowhere is such a practice more persistent than in a family. It is almost a universal practice (although less than in the past) to adopt different standards when raising boy as opposed to girls. Some practices are acceptable for boys, others are condoned for girls. This is not about natural genetic, chromosomal, or hormonal differences and their impact. There are some built-in stereotypic reactions. Often the girls grow up with the understanding that such and such a career is not for her. Many girls grow up and have to make a conscious effort to come out of the box where they were placed while being raised at home. The ideal environment must be able to provide the same opportunity for boys and girls and allow them to expand to the maximum of their potential and ability.

At home, a young girl, as well as a young boy, must learn good manners and how to dress. Both must be equally stimulated to become mature enough to have enough confidence in their abilities and their decisions. It is no longer acceptable to raise girls to become somebody's wife, while neglecting her education, her well-being, and her ability to compete at any comparable level with anyone, be it a man or woman. It is also clear that the other extreme must also be avoided. The parents must examine their value systems and overcome any type of bias or prejudice.

The masculine stereotype

Although this is the postmodern era, the mistakes and misconception of the past will not disappear overnight. For millennia, society has favored men over women. Despite the reported progress, we are functioning in a world that is still dominated by men. The judiciary, executive, legislative systems, and various private sectors are still disproportionately filled with men. The woman who wants to make it in this male-dominated world ought not to be or feel intimidated. She must know when to go around a given obstacle and when to fight discrimination in the business world. She must learn and know how and when to pick a fight. She must also take advantage of what she brings to the work place, even in political settings: a practical approach to problem solving, a sense and necessity for transparency, a nurturing approach to the various problems, and better understanding of many issues, such as children's day care, health care, social services, employment, civil rights, family, the elderly, education, etc.

By the same token, you must at least question the pattern of behavior that is conventionally acceptable, when it is about the sexual and sentimental approach. It is time for a woman to realize it is not shameful for her to initiate a romantic relationship. A man must be mature enough not to feel threatened if she makes the first move. There are quite a few changes to be made in the socio-political, financial, and sentimental structures.

The woman's responsibilities

Under scrutiny

An examination of how to bring the scale to its equilibrium leads also to the analysis of the woman's role in moving forward and changing the situation. There is a symbiotic relationship between men and women. A man's role is defined in relation to a woman's role, and vice versa. The behavior of one often triggers some responses from the other. The message can be misunderstood. Therefore, it is worth making it as clear as possible. Men and women are equal but not identical. The woman's emancipation is not a diploma to become a man. Rudeness, vulgarity, aggressiveness, and an antagonistic approach do not cut it for anyone. No one has the green light to misbehave. Two wrongs do not make one right. A woman who is living in this world is able to find a way to excel, to produce with devotion, dedication perseverance, but also with wisdom, honesty, and tact. No need to rub it in. Her presence, her appearance should neither be a threat nor a source of distraction. She must impose respect and clean comradeship. You can be firm and independent without being obnoxious. You can be graceful and grateful while remaining focused on the target and the ultimate goal.

There are times also when you need to be aggressive or ruthless to reach your goal. As a consistent, professional woman, you know how to behave in a working environment. You will not get involved in gossip, back stabbing, loud laughter, mood swings, lunatic humor, sexual turn-ons, or a long list of bad habits that your enemies—who are likely goading you to behave in such a way—will gladly use against you. You must be careful not to become your own worst enemy in hampering your well-deserved ascending progress. There should be no hostility, no war between a man and a woman. Instead, apply a calm, collected, gender-blind, sensible, and constructive approach with your head above your shoulders. This is the key to dissipating tension and fostering cooperation for everyone's success.

Guilt complex

Because so much is expected and required from you as a woman, you tend to spread yourself too thin and may become vulnerable. Today's world is witnessing many changes at a pace faster than many can keep track of. Therefore, the consequences are multifaceted. One of the domains where changes are not necessarily for the best is at the level of the family. The family is undergoing tremendous pressures. With all the changes in the trend of life, the rate of failure in families is climbing. Women often feel guilty when their families fall apart. This is the time to point out that you are not responsible for things that you cannot control. The key is always to be sure you have done your best to avoid a catastrophic outcome. Many professionals can attest to the fact that mothers come to the office clearly devastated. Why? Their child, who was such a promising kid, turned out to be using drugs, or no longer wants to go to school, or is engaged in all kinds of marginal activities. You must remember that the conditions that govern a child's choices are multi-faceted.

When people are young, there is an innate desire to go ahead and do their own thing and try to acquire their own experiences. Unfortunately, they often choose to listen to and follow their friends. They tend to rebel against established principles of the home. Do not blame yourself; you know that you did all that was within your power for your child. You also shouldn't feel guilty if you attempted to save your marriage, and your partner just walked out. Did you do your best? The heavens took note of it. It is time to cut the chain of unnecessary culpability, face all guilt, and move on. No human creature was given the role to carry all the burdens on this earth. You should not take it upon yourself to change the world at the snap of your fingers. Everyone has his own load; do the best you can.

It is clear that the current generation sees the feminine presence in various domains and levels that used to be forbidden to women not too long ago. We see women on television, the Internet, in education, publicity, advertising, communication, health care, pharmacy, hospitality, commerce, the military, etc. However, you need to realize that the road ahead is long and tortuous. If you want to succeed, you must not rest on your laurels. You need to remain vibrant, vigilant, confident, skillful, and even aggressive. You should never hesitate to further your education and qualifications. You have an objective, and it is clearly written and stated. You are highly motivated. You show courage, thoroughness, and perseverance. You have a game plan. You are willing to educate yourself and gather the resources and knowledge needed. You have a strategy. You know what steps to take. You hide behind no excuses. You hold no grudges. You accept help from anyone who genuinely wants to help without strings attached. You are willing and able to make the appropriate behavioral and lifestyle changes. You learn from your mistakes. You know how to change challenges into opportunities. You are on the move. Better yet, you have some unique advantages: You have good insight, compassion, thoroughness, empathy, and sympathy. You look out for the benefit of your clients and your community. You love to get involved with your community. You embrace changes and exploit them advantageously instead of fighting them. You can decide on your own your profession and choose a lifestyle that is convenient for you. You need advice, but you must decide for your own. You are responsible for your soul. You can help and guide others within the realm of your possibilities. You are entitled to make your choices and face the consequences. Watch out man… here comes the woman making strides. It is catch-up time!

In this world of "deconstruction" that seems to wander away, you must accumulate many passions with a commitment that is to last all your life. As you live in this century, the call is to action.

- Take inventory of your assets and count and appreciate your accomplishments: the right to stay or get out of an unbearable relationship; the right to have control of your reproductive organs; the right to decide on your fertility, your sexuality; the right to have equal opportunity for a diversified education; the right to obtain a salary that corresponds with your qualifications and your performance, to take a loan under your own name; the possibility to apply for and obtain any public function; and the right to build your financial autonomy.

- Identify what is left to fight for and the resources available. Beware of the complexity of the current world. You must have a hierarchy of priorities and also choose a plan to operate and get the results needed. Among the challenges you can name, a few are: ability to reconcile family life and professional life without feeling guilty; accept gracefully the role of being the main breadwinner for your family; identify areas of discrimination, such as employment, salaries, careers, authentic equality, and political access.

Fight for feminine dignity, against pornography, woman's body exploitation, prostitution, domestic and institutional violence, wearing a veil forcefully, and getting married unwillingly. Fight for women's equal opportunities in education and physical and mental health. See to it that the advantages and rights already obtained are not eroded. Yet through it all, remain graceful and cordial.

All in all, a woman is a human being equal but different from a man. You contribute greatly to the society, and it is time for your contribution to be acknowledged. You are not an object, not a thing, not a slave. You are entitled to the same rights, privileges, protections, and treatments that your counterpart obtains. You deserve a job compatible with your level of qualifications and competency. You deserve equal pay for equal work. The promotions and opportunities must be as accessible to you as they are to the other party, who supposedly is mature enough not to be intimidated, skeptical, or immature. Anywhere you can function and operate as a human being, you deserve the respect, salary, and treatment that go with your status. No one should confound politeness with weakness, flexibility with manipulation. Of course this is an uphill battle that requires the help of everyone. Collaboration and understanding are welcome. This is a global challenge. Together it can be done.

Minorities and Success

Stumbling Blocks to Minorities' Success

"The most certain test by which we judge whether a country is really free is the amount of security enjoyed by minorities" (Lord Acton, *"The History of Freedom in Antiquity"*, 1877).

There are over 7,500 ethnic and minority communities in the world. This number includes racial, religious, and political groups that are fewer in number and different from the majority of people that compose a nation. The current demographic makeup of our society counts diverse racial and ethnic groups. This takes into consideration not only some immutable characteristics, such as skin, complexion, hair texture, and outward appearance, but also some features such as cultures, traditions, languages, social interpretations, and classification that can be acquired or altered. The level of dependency, influence, and incremental progress of these minority groups depend on the dynamism, power, and resources of the majority groups; their public policy decisions; obvious or covert actions; conspiracy; and restrictive covenants imposed.

Regardless of your race, it is inherent to human beings to move toward social categorization, racial division, class membership, and power struggle. It is an innate human tendency that when you are in command, you'd rather act according to the limit of your power, get carried away toward a lack of self-control, instead of governing by reason or fairness. If you have everything under your control, you automatically believe it is because you are better and bigger. You want to stay on top in the human hierarchy, and you do not accept any threat to your hegemony. You naturally see your group, your class, your race as superior to the others. You rule, make policies, and judge the world around you based on your viewpoint, and you want the others to accept the laws that you set yourself.

Let us consider the United States of America, for example. History tells us that the founders were a majority of religiously and ethnically diverse white people. The nation evolved through periods of slavery, settlement, segregation, civil war, and internment camp. As a result, there has been discrimination in many domains, including education, employment, and housing, and even in the government. Because groups tend to be in opposition to one another, because the majority of the people were whites, initially such discrimination was basically racial, between whites and nonwhites. The white majority naturally enacted laws, regulations, and policies that were in their favor and according to the models they knew from the old world Europeans' example: colonization, slavery, exploitations. The results were obvious: power and wealth for the majority, who happened to be whites in the United States of America; subordination and exploitation for the nonwhite minorities. Because the majority (ethnically diverse whites) had hegemony, they believed that they race must be intrinsically superior. This is racism. With a constant struggle for dominance, there is abuse, injustice, violence, discrimination, marginalization, bigotry, prejudice, hatred, and propaganda: anything to keep the minorities where they are. When generations after generations keep hearing derogatory remarks about their group, their race, they wind up believing them. Do not be surprised if they show self-hatred, if they do not want to do much, because they have been programmed with negative thoughts. How can they trust such a system? How can you talk to them about fairness, loyalty, self-confidence, self-determination? When another group keeps hearing how wonderful all of its people are, they believe it. They are motivated to outdo themselves—and with the help of the others who have no rights to get any credits for anything they do—the sky is the limit. The result is stereotyping.

Two women (one white, one nonwhite) give birth to two healthy babies. The white baby has the best environment possible, he goes to school, and everything is available for him. The nonwhite upon his birth is a burden. As a child of a slave woman, he cannot learn how to write and read. He has the bare minimum to survive to become another slave at the mercy of the white majority. It does not take a rocket scientist to figure out whose descendants are likely to make it, according to this world's criteria

Even centuries later, those minorities, such as African-Americans, Native Americans, Latin Americans, Asians, and other immigrant groups, continue to suffer the consequences and perceive racism in their day-to-day dealing. Skin color remains a factor, in many instances, that hampers one's access to several opportunities. Many cases of blatant racism show no reasoning, but just pure emotion and deeply rooted prejudice, taught generation after generation. It is fair to say that the attitude of racism is present in almost every group toward some other groups. It is safe to say that the race card alone does not explain fully and immutably the question of poverty or of failure.

People attuned to the current general situation can also note the tendency to lump together the issues of racism, minorities, wealth, and class struggle. But in reality, these notions are not synonymous. Although a full discussion on these issues is beyond the scope of this book, it is worth attempting to untwist those threads. Poverty knows no boundaries and does not discriminate. Wealth does not refuse to enter into the house of someone, just because of his color or age or gender. Many factors commingle to define the living condition of people. For example, two people can be classified as poor based on their income. But one may have parents to rely on every now and then, while the other has no parent or family member he can turn to; one may have a better education that can eventually facilitate his move forward. A number of factors determine the success of a given ethnic or racial group.

The issue of class struggle also is often agitated as the source of inequalities. Let us consider the current situation. We know of many examples of people who have climbed up the ladder despite all odds to the contrary. People are not precipitously dumped into a lower class or propelled into a higher one. Those so-called classes are not sealed to keep the people out or to keep people in until the end. There is no formal hereditary caste. The upper, middle, and lower classes are usually determined based on income and wealth. But because there has been a culture of wealth in a given group, and poverty in another, the result is a reflection of what has been practiced for centuries. The economic dynamic determines where you fall or stand. Any class can have any color, age, gender, or creed. In the land of free enterprise, everyone is allowed to find an independent way to survive. There is no bourgeois or proletariat dictatorship; the economy dictates the market. Contrary to Karl Marx's prediction, we have not seen two more and more polarized classes. Again, public policies, economic parameters, interest rates, inflation, and unemployment are likely to weigh a lot more in the class migration upward or downward. Income, education, opportunity, family assets, values, motivation, intergenerational relations, and transfer of wealth, identity, language, beliefs, and culture are all integrated to make the difference.

If a black person becomes the CEO of a corporation, his primarily goal is to maximize the profit of that corporation at the minimum cost. Therefore, he will take all the necessary measures to reach his goal, including paying the minimum allowed to the employees, whether they are black or white or yellow. Is that black CEO an oppressor, a racist, or is he playing with the economic parameters available to him?

As a matter of fact, even among a given population—black people for example—there seems to be a class divide that is based on priorities, values, ethics, environment, beliefs, education, and the level of interaction with other groups and races. Some may go as far as talking about segregation among black people, because—with different objectives—somehow they have grown apart and been exposed to different challenges, even though apparently they belong to the same race, they have different interests and want to pursue different objectives. The trend is toward focusing on a global set of values that help people to blend in and become part of the mainstream of the nation. The new generation seems to grow closer despite racial or ethnic differences. Nevertheless, people must remember who they are, so they will not be disappointed when they reach a gateway where one group may inherently have more difficulties to go through compared to the other.

Although the current dichotomy between rich and poor has a racial tone, the economic divide is not solely due to race, but also related to history. When the rich exploit the poor, they would have exploited them anyway, regardless of race, because the rich are in the business of staying rich and they are willing to take any steps necessary to stay that way. Again, the relationship between wealth and poverty does not hinge on race per se, but on economic variables and history.

It is important not to confuse race with class or wealth. The difference does exist.

Imagine a marathon. Two women are well prepared to run it. Once the marathon starts, one of the women is allowed to run, the other one has to untangle all kinds of administrative red tape and distractions. Finally she is free to go after the first woman, who is already halfway through the race.

What is the chance for both to reach the finish line together? In the meantime, the public is not even aware of the reasons why the second woman came up to the race so late. It is clear that civil rights, affirmative action, private sector organizations, education, and communication have helped toward restoring the equilibrium. But the road remains long. In this twenty-first century, it is clear that institutionalized obvious discrimination is officially banished. But its ramification, its stratification has not yet vanished. Statistics prove there is a considerable gap between the wealthy and the poor. Further analysis will give you a wide gap between whites' and blacks' shares of wealth. The issue is multidimensional; it is not as simple as it may seem. It is not just whites versus blacks, poor versus rich, minority versus majority. For example, the Jews are not black, yet they are minority. As a matter of fact, they constitute less than five percent of the population, compared to the black population. Yet the Jews play a dominant role in academia, politics, sciences, economics, arts, Nobel Prizes, etc. How can such a small group have such big influence and so much wealth?

This forces us to study the issue more carefully and more deeply. America is a national mosaic, made up of whites, blacks, Hispanics, Asians, Pacific Islanders, Native Americans, etc. Even among each group there are nuances, differences. So, why does one group belong to the have-nots and another group belongs to the haves? The Jewish group is really fascinating. They seem to lead everywhere they go. The sixty-four million dollar question is why? Could it be because of religious culture and traditions, family core values and principles, including self-confidence, encouraging creativity, entrepreneurship and high expectations, lessons learned from history, including the bad experiences, solidarity, discipline, innate driving spirit to go further, yet be prudent and vigilant? Is it race or is it history, culture? Think about it!

When it comes to black people, or more precisely, when we have to talk about the relationship between blacks and whites, there is at least some uneasiness. Both sides seem to be reluctant to have a candid, practical, but respectful discussion. There are past events and actions that people do not feel comfortable to discuss, yet everyone talks about forgiving and forgetting. To have closure, there must be dialogue, repentance, and forgiveness. The best way to avoid further discord is to let history speak for itself. Unfortunately, not too many people know or accept history. How about some simple questions? During the 1800s, when land ownership was accessible only to citizens, since black people were not considered as citizens, did they also have such a privilege? In the 1950s most people of color were domestic and agricultural workers; didn't the New Deal and Social Security exclude domestic and agricultural workers? How many veterans of color could benefit from the GI Bill? When VA and FHA prevented mortgages in mixed-race and urban neighborhoods, who tended to be affected the most? When student loans became no longer tax deductible, who are more likely not to have a parent to help them through education? When private landing institutions and real estate agents redlined some areas and practically ignored them or served them at a higher interest rate, who was likely to suffer by seeing the values of those properties go down? Who are likely not to be able to own a home? If a black person and white person lose their respective economic footings, which one is likely to go and find a safety net from parents or family members to hold on to until the storm is over? Furthermore, which one is likely to get back on his feet faster? The chance for the white person's assets and wealth to come from him and him alone, without parents or family members providing assistance, is less than that of the black person, who has to start on his own in a system where the values, standards, and policies are set by the majority. Some people may need to be convinced by the written history. Let us read the special message to the Congress by the thirty-seventh president of the United States on March19, 1972: "…In recent years, we have done much to press open new doors of opportunity for millions of Americans to whom those doors had previously been barred, or only half open. In jobs, housing, education, old obstacles are being removed. But for Blacks, Mexican Americans, Puerto Ricans, Indians and other minorities who have known discrimination, economic opportunity must also increasingly be made to mean a greater chance to know the satisfactions, the rewards and the responsibilities of business ownership. Such opportunities are not only important in themselves; they also help make possible the economic and social advances that are critical to the development of stable and thriving communities on which the social and economic vitality of the Nation as a whole depend…" Do you believe President Nixon knew what he was talking about? If so, he was stating the facts, whether we like it or not. Now, it is paramount to know how to find ways, develop policies, and adopt a politic of engagement, flexibility in all levels and every domain in order to build trust, positive attitude. The government must actively develop policies to level the playing field as its top priority. Instead of lowering standards, there should be easy access to more training, remedial education matched by an eagerness to learn. There should be equal opportunity in learning and training and promoting with fair assignment and treatment. People should be taught to eliminate stereotypes, prejudicial jokes, generalized negative comments, and demeaning remarks. A sense of responsibility, high self-esteem, critical thinking, and high expectation from all should be the motto. No one wants to get into a position and then wonder whether or not he made it because of some special favor. Instead, he should have equal access and opportunity to work on his weak spots and get on with his life. Education should be encouraged for all, in all fields, including science, mathematics, and engineering, with resources and challenges to do better each time because the effort will be equally appreciated. Counseling should target people to work on their inborn abilities, coupled with their adaptability, instead of directing some people to liberal arts while discouraging them from medicine or law or engineering. Undergraduate and graduate education should not be limited only to those who can afford it. There should be no undeclared conspiracy to make it easy for one group and difficult for the others. Housing, mortgages, various types of loans are all affected by public and private policies. Policies also should develop to strengthen families. Cultural diversity should be not feared but embraced, because it provides richness and variety of choice. When anyone in any group perceives the other to be genuinely making an effort to improve the situation, when the attitude is positive, when there is a frank dialogue to find solutions together and not at the expense of the other, interracial, interethnic, intercultural tensions will at least diminish and produce a positive domino effect.

The issues of education, employment, social and cultural groups, family matters, gender roles, relationship between generations, and identity obviously remind us all that there is a multidimensional approach to such a thorny question as equality versus inequality, minorities versus majorities. The questions of fairness, integration, and identity must take into consideration the uniqueness of each component while adding it to the whole nation. The idea of unity and equal opportunity within diversity is not easy to implement. After all, the key question remains how to maintain the greatness, the wealth of a nation, while fostering the advancement of every group. We need knowledge of history, understanding, and insight into human diversity, all working toward such a goal, but practically, people are different and naturally biased. Government has its role to play. When equal effort matches equal opportunity, then motivation, desire to achieve, family wealth, education, a positive view of accessibility to full human potentiality and having it count make the difference. Socioeconomic progress depends upon public policy. Wealth depends upon the assets, means, the revenues, the resources, the values, and, again, government policies. Wealth also has its impact on health, education, and available opportunities.

Of course, there is much rhetoric and a myriad of viewpoints, but we must keep the dialogue going. The "sink or swim," "achievements only" approach will not cut it; a handout won't do it either. People's behavior acquired through many factors and over years and through generations cannot disappear overnight. The expected behavior of someone is likely to make him act accordingly. All in all, the ultimate goal is to live in a world where people are blindfolded and judge others based on their merit, with equal privileges, rights, and opportunities. Obviously we are not there yet; therefore, public and private sectors should take steps to foster such changes through laws and policies, dialogue, communication, solidarity, commitment, self-determination, peaceful coexistence, and integration instead of segregation or ghetto-ization, and should verify incremental progress. A candid commission on racial harmony should not be ruled out, even if it may appear politically incorrect. People in all groups and camps should stop thinking about denigrating each other or fostering hierarchical relationships, where the dominant party calls all the shots. It is time for integration, fairness, and opportunities for all, not as separate entities in constant collision with each other, but as a nation, a world working together and simultaneously on many fronts toward a fairer and more balanced society. If we do not do it for us, at least let us do it for the next generation.

The Role of Minorities in Their Own Success

How many times have you been obsessed by an idea, but for some reason—the fear of failing, the fear of being laughed at by friends and foes—you just dump it in the morgue to join the long list of your unfulfilled dreams? Then you experience a pang of loss, like a woman who suffers a miscarriage. You cannot ignore the matriarchal character of success. Nothing can match a living experience. If it is good, it propels you all the way to the top to challenge the heavens, and you feel your best; your energy is flowing through and through. But if it is a bad experience, you feel flat, like a frog that someone just stepped on. Among the people who do not make it are those who are paralyzed by the idea of failing. Some are not even sure that they should be successful. They lose all the strength and desire to try again, although they could have been successful the next time.

Success depends on factors that coalesce to form a whole in which the diverse ingredients are barely visible individually. When you happen to succeed, you have been able to blend together your goals, your plans, your fears, your emotions, your ambitions, and your trials, along with your potential to make it. You live in a unique world where your dreams take shape and form through your determination and action, even though a reality check around you would have convinced you otherwise. You take a leap of faith, and you are already living that dream.

The decision to get through makes you a dreamer who is willing to conquer what others believe is inaccessible.

Galileo lost his life because he refused to give up something he was convinced of, although by human criteria he might have seemed crazy. What differentiates a crazy person from a dreamer? The crazy person constantly lives in an unreal world; he lives in his dreams. The one who is bound to succeed dreams his life. The lunatic, drags a life of static, passive dreams. The one who is to succeed, lives a dynamic life. The former dreams with his eyes tightly closed, while the latter dreams with eyes wide open and constantly moving.

Success can be found only by those who seek it. Man is the first maker and fabricator of his destiny. Many times success is almost touchable, but the waiting appears to take forever. You give up, you sell out and discover that somebody else just takes off with what you fought so hard to get. He took it where you left off and makes it at your expense. When discouragement and despair get hold of you, they blur your vision and obstruct your sight, so that you can no longer appreciate the enlightened approach to success. Although the environment plays its role in your success, it is strongly dependent on your choices and validated through your actions. The key depends on your capacity to endure trials and tribulations, your ability to persevere and to learn from your past mistakes. Your level of success depends on the degree of your ambition and motivation. Anytime someone is mad at the whole world, blames everybody for his misfortunes, and has an excuse for each of his shortcomings, he is digging his hole of failures much deeper and may even drag someone else with him. You cannot succeed if you just talk about success and get jealous of those who make it, but never express what you want in life or how you plan to get there. Nobody is going to make it for you. Most people are out there to make it for themselves. So if you want it, stop talking about it, pull up your sleeves, and start working toward it.

It is like someone who keeps dreaming of a great meal for Sunday but has no clue as to what constitutes a great meal or how or where he is going to get it. Before you get around a lovely table to eat, the food and ingredients must be obtained and prepared by someone who knows how to do it. The first step entails a mental revolution. There's got to be a conscientious awareness that the current situation is not acceptable. You must develop the capacity to distance yourself from your own self and take stock of the situation.

It is time to unlearn all the fallacies that you learned while growing up. This includes the idea that it is impossible to obtain success, some people just cannot do it, or that whatever happens was bound to happen, or people are against you and want to keep you down. Even if they do, be determined to prove them wrong. Get rid of this negative brainwashing. Nothing can stop a tenacious, success-bound human being.

For example, what do we think about wealthy people? How do you look at their wealth? Is it with a suspicious eye? Are you wondering what illicit acts they must have done to get there? Some believe that rich people get their wealth from exploiting poor defenseless people, manipulating circumstances, taking advantage of many occasions, and finding ways to avoid paying their fair share of taxes. Whether this belief is true or not, thinking that way violates two principles:

- You should not generalize, nor should you take a blanket approach to life, in which you put everyone in the same basket. This is biased, counterproductive, and wrong.

- When you internalize such an idea about wealthy people, the rich person becomes the detested villain. And therefore, consciously or unconsciously, you cannot stand being rich and you opt for poverty, because you would not be yourself had you been rich. Therefore, you are living a self-fulfilled prophecy; you are caught in a vicious cycle and in a state of denial. Later on if you do not watch yourself, you may become jealous and irritated by the wealthy, for no reason other than the fact that he or she is rich. It is even more critical than that, because you may become very angry against him or her without even knowing why. Unconsciously, you are pulled toward the status quo and you reject prosperity. Your inner self is telling you to stay poor. This is what you know; this is your comfort zone; generally, changes bring anxiety and apprehension.

How are you going to get something that your brain and your self-awareness have rejected already? This is like the unfortunate scenario where your own immune system rejects a transplant that is vital for your survival.

You spend your entire life wanting to be rich or have a better way of life; yet if you mentally can't stand the wealthy people around you, you cannot make it, because the mind and the heart are not there. If you want to improve your condition of life, if you intend to get wealthy, you must consider all the good deeds wealth can facilitate and vow to make the difference when you get there. Everything depends upon your thought process.

A little eagle that spent most of his life among chickens, behaved like a chicken. But one day an eagle who was passing by made an emergency landing, and he talked to the eagle who was behaving like a chicken. He had a tough time convincing the other eagle that he was not a chicken but a strong eagle that could fly high into the sky. It took the eagle a lot of work to convince the other and help him identify what he really was. It took the little eagle some time just to realize what the big eagle was telling him, and then the rest depends on the choice of the little eagle.

Sometimes it is difficult to discover the truth and accept it. But once you do, you are free to fly away and go conquer what you were destined to conquer all along. After that little eagle found out about his potential, he had the choice to start flying like an eagle, prefer the quiet life of a chicken, or even start bickering and fighting and blaming all the chickens for holding him back for so long. Again, ultimately the choice is yours! It is clear that for many people, life is saturated with all sorts of privation. The ultimate outcome depends on how these problems are addressed and how emotions and frustrations are managed.

In a mixed society, where different races, ethnicities, and factions evolve, there is a dynamic influence that is constantly pushing and pulling to give more influence or territory to one group at the expense of another. It requires some fair guidelines to prevent disaster. The dynamism created by the cohabitation of all these different people imposes a constant declared or undeclared fight to dominate. When you really think about it, everyone belongs to some minority, everyone is potentially oppressed or bullied by someone or something. The key is to confront it when it is appropriate, but never let it stop you from moving forward. Do not allow yourself to be paralyzed by it. In the western world, for instance, true power is not necessarily defined according to the number of people reported by the Census Bureau. Instead, the weight goes where the money is. The groups of people who have the most money have a bigger share of the pie. These people are therefore able to control the events, decide the predominant issues, and take all the necessary steps to protect their interests and obtain the maximum return on investment and maintain control of the situation. This group is not necessarily the majority of the population. It can be a small group that leads the rest of the world. That same small group may have enough influence to lobby in favor of its positions. Obviously these people will do their best to control the situation for as long as possible. This can be anyone, any group, any ethnicity, any race in power. We all like to enjoy some privileges for as long as it is possible. In such a scenario, the minorities who do not have the ways and means to relay influence must either accept the situation as it is, or play dead or protest and maybe revolt. But whatever they do, they must always be aware of the consequences that do not necessarily go their way. Everything is possible at the proper time and within the right circumstances.

The wise move is often a compromise. In a mixed society, the party in power takes the steps to stay in power as much as it can. Some have enough tact to make the rest of the people feel less uncomfortable; others are rough and aggressive and make the situation tenser than it should be.

Because of man's gregarious instinct to survive, he is naturally inclined to do whatever is to his best interest, and this may be at the expense of others. The moment he is in power, he is willing to take all the steps possible and use all kinds of gimmicks to stay in power: nepotism, gerontocracy, oligarchy, dictatorship, or totalitarianism. He can surround himself by a loyal clique that is susceptible to help him maintain economic, political, legislative, judiciary, and executive power. This gives him enough clout to protect whatever he already acquired and to pose himself in a position for other privileges. He should be highly motivated to keep the status quo and to maintain law and order, peace, security, and stability for the community and the country.

But sometimes the familiarity of power breeds corruption, and he begins to look after his own interests at the expense of the people he should represent and defend. If man is generally defined according to cultural, social, philosophical, juridical, religious, psychological, and political factors, the minority groups are no exception. Nevertheless, based on the geographical location where they are posted, some members of minority groups often have felt reduced to the level of the weak link in the vast human chain. After generations have gone through such gimmicks, where parents, grandparents, and great grandparents have all been conditioned and brainwashed to accommodate a given class, how do you see success? How are you ever going to pierce through the thick shield of poverty? You are asked to go to school and educate yourself, while at the same time you feel that everything is put in place for you not to find any channel possible through which you can succeed. Everything is so expensive and you cannot afford it. If through some miracle you acquire a good education, you see yourself being forced to take a position that is far below your qualifications and credentials, in order to survive and start paying back your student loan. It is a vicious cycle. What do you do? Again, you are not asking for a handout. All you want is a level playing field. Human life takes a dynamic dimension and depends upon your capacity to adapt to various factors. Everyone has the right to seek happiness and to benefit from certain privileges. Leisure time and pleasures are part of everyone's agenda. You want to travel, to go on vacation, have fun, and be prosperous. Unfortunately, many times you have to postpone the vacation; you keep hoping for a better tomorrow while wondering if it will ever come. Again, we must bear in mind this can happen to anyone in any group, but the reasons are diverse and unique for each. A peaceful solution to such a conflict becomes very difficult to swallow for many. Those who consider themselves victims of abuse want changes and they cannot wait forever. It is evident that the definition of success for the oppressed is not going to be the same as for the oppressors. Nevertheless, because mankind was born with the flame of freedom burning inextinguishably within, the underserved, the disadvantaged, will always ask why they are the ones in such predicament and will not rest until the conditions changed for them.

This can manifest itself in various ways:

- The entrenched belief that whatever is part of the oppressed is inferior or worthless: for example, some oppressed people subconsciously want to look like the oppressor: skin whitening, long hair braids, lip surgery, etc.

- The systematic rejection of anything that reminds the oppressed of the oppressors: customs, ways to get dressed, to speak, to walk, to reason, to behave, etc. Yet the oppressed do not have other examples to follow. So what can be done? They tend to develop a pattern that is systematically the opposite from the oppressors. For those who have been exploited, their freedom is measured by the categorical rejection of whatever can remind them of the other people. Even after they have made some progress, they still feel the yokes on them. They feel what you may call phantom oppression, like the patient who continues to suffer from the pain stemming from a limb that was already amputated, yet still hurts.

For the underprivileged groups, the system that prevents them from moving up is still in place, even though, theoretically, all measures are taken to grant them equality in every aspect of life. In many cases, the psychological chains are more cumbersome than the physical ones. The first dilemma for minorities is often their inability to find a way to exploit their freedom. Once they realize that they are free from psychological and physical oppression, many assume they must enjoy that freedom. Enjoying their freedom may be defined as no more hard work, no more structures, no more hierarchy. It is time for relaxation, partying, and enjoying life. Yet in reality, newly acquired freedom is fragile. It goes hand-in-hand with more hard work, more discipline, and more difficulties, especially in the beginning. It is like the deep and heavy darkness before dawn. Some want a revolutionary approach to everything, in order to mark their differences from the oppressors of the past, whereby they reject anything that is susceptible of reminding them of oppression and discrimination. On the other side, they must face the reality of their daily life, where they have basically nothing—no structure and no foundation— to build on. The only system in place is the one from the so-called enemies who perpetuate their condition. How much choice do they have? They must be careful not to isolate themselves and cause strangulation of their entire group. The healthy approach is to avoid a generalized blanket approach, in which everyone who is not part of your group is one of them and therefore against you. The other side of this philosophy is holding grudges that prevent advancement and constructive actions. Disadvantaged people must be open enough to accept help from anyone who is genuinely interested in their well-being and their progress.

If human subjectivism tends to classify people according to their phenotypic appearances, the practical life requires a different approach. There is no inexorable cleavage between different classes, sectors, countries, or the world in general. This is not a caste society. The classification of people cannot be exclusively made based on skin appearance. Many people obviously belong to a certain race, ethnicity, or class; but in actuality they belong to that given group only apparently or when there is a declared threat that can be avoided through their apparent identity, or when their interests or survival are at stake.

The distinction among people, as to who belongs to what, is not as easy as you may think. It is not theoretical, but practical. Those who espouse the cause of the poor, the underserved, and the exploited do not always belong to one specific group. As a matter of fact, outsiders may make a world of difference when they have clout and they are willing to help. Remember, Martin Luther King, Jr., had other people who sympathized with him and participated in his struggle for freedom and social justice. Again, minorities do not necessarily mean those who are poor or miserable. Those who are disadvantaged must be willing to welcome those from other camps who genuinely want to help them. This is a sign of maturity. Being illusory, irritable, angry, antagonistic, and destructive is not mature.

Again, those who belong to a given group must not have a blanket approach, whereby everyone is judged by their appearances and their belongings. Everyone deserves at least the benefit of the doubt until he proves himself through concrete deeds. The toughest pill to swallow is to realize the criteria, the values, and the system in which things were developed centuries ago, often by the ancestors of those who have been known to condone and benefit from oppression and inequality.

Are the oppressed going to get into the arena of the oppressors to confront them by playing the same game with the same rules put in place by the wealthy referees? This is not an easy choice; it requires serious considerations. It also opens a window into the minorities' world of obstacles and stressors. This is an ever-present situation. The people in power pass the laws and set the rules; name the judges, lawyers, and law enforcement agents; and build the jails. The disadvantaged sometimes feel trapped and question every aspect of life, every system that is in place, including judiciary and legislative systems. The best way to solve this problem is to do what is best all the time and to remember that it takes time to persevere and see the expected changes with their results.

Besides, those in power also have their own problems to deal with. Many among them are against all types of abuse and injustice. They sincerely want to see the emancipation of those who were denied some basic rights and privileges; nevertheless, deep inside there is the survival instinct that makes them at least nervous as to the cost of such emancipation. The instinct of self-preservation naturally makes you fearful and cautious. The unknown often makes you worrisome. Without doubting their good faith, those people also want to make sure of their own survival, as well as the survival of their loved ones and their offspring. Everyone wants the same things: safety, stability, prosperity, and perpetuity. Since things are scarce and limited, whoever gets them first wants to hold on to them. Otherwise, there is no guarantee there will be enough for all. No one wants to kill himself to save others. You can help to a certain extent, without endangering your own future. Furthermore, when the members of a given group want to help another, they automatically become suspect in the eyes of their own people. They must be careful and tactful; otherwise they run the risk of being rebuked and kicked out by their own. It is a tightrope.

The majorities and the minorities must exploit their common and strong desires to succeed and start the dialogue. The emphasis should be on common interests, not on what divides us. The rhetoric of superiority, domination, inferiority, and exploitation must be at least toned down and eventually eliminated. The focus should be on the innate attraction to help others, to understand each other, to make this world a better place for us and for generations to come. At a time when the differences between those who have and those who have not do not seem to improve to a satisfactory level, we must have a moratorium to find ways to help everyone, or in the end we will all have a lot to lose. There must be a mechanism put in place to come to the rescue of those who are dying of hunger, disease, political instability, insecurity, and natural disaster. The higher your position, the bigger your means, and the greater are your responsibilities. What may seem paradoxical is nevertheless very pragmatic.

You cannot be successful until you have helped another brother who lies in abject poverty to become self-sufficient. After all, we are all journeying together toward the same finitude. Your true value rests upon your contribution to your society. There comes a moment in your life where the dignity and well-being of your neighbor have a direct impact on your own well-being; it is worth helping your neighbor. By so doing you help yourself as well. Nevertheless, the help provided must not be conceived or received by either party as an entitlement or a little charity. It should be met with some effort, determination, and understanding on both sides.

Another big hurdle toward minorities' advancement is the behavior within a given group among themselves. This is the elephant in the room that no one wants to talk about. Members are mistreated, physically and emotionally abused by their own people, the same ones who were supposed to help them and look out for them. When this happens, they are taken off guard and feel victimized twice. When certain people of a given group adopt a self-destructive behavior, very little can be done with such conduct. You can take people out of poverty, ignorance, and self-destruction, but you cannot take the poverty, ignorance, and self-destruction out of the people. You should not try to destroy those who are trying to help you. You should not pretend to help while you are hurting and harming, either. Anger is a lethal weapon of self-destruction for anyone. Individuals look up and see the mountains to climb, a multiplicity of challenges to face, the lack of support from their own people is the last straw to push them to despair. They feel trapped, and many choose to give up and declare themselves defeated victims. They just surrender and take refuge in the tomb of inertia. When you hear this initially, you may think they have reason, because they have some solid arguments to make their case. However, you must remember this goes against the fundamental principles of living. Life is a journey. It is a big puzzle, but it is also a packed parade. Everyone must move; life in inertia is inconceivable.

If you refuse to move, you may move backward or be crushed by the crowd or be thrown away by the high waves and the strong winds that come in. Inertia is sometime conceived as laziness. This never figures on the list of those who want to succeed. It is a force that can destroy the whole structure of success. All opportunities are meaningless when we face the iceberg of inertia. It puts a hole on the screen of success and removes the wheels of progress. That approach makes you a member of the zero-risk-for-success club. You are only willing to fight and advance on such a road under one condition: you want an unequivocal guarantee of the results you are seeking. But that doesn't work. No pain, no gain. If people could have the absolute certainty that what they invest in will bring them ample profits, such a principle would have been universally endorsed and practiced. After all, when we take an airplane from point A to point B, we would love the guarantee of making it there safely and on time. Even when we go to war, we would love the guarantee of winning overnight, with limited cost and zero casualties. Unfortunately, our cosmic life has a lot of risks. The higher the risk, the bigger is the reward. The level of success is directly proportional to the rate of risk and the degree of effort.

Nothing certifies that any decisions taken or any of the various approaches are going to land you on a pile of gold or diamonds. You always face a risk that your chosen course may lead to failure. But if you choose to do nothing, you are guaranteed to get nowhere and may even move backward. Take into consideration the choices, the possible outcomes, the alternatives, the possibilities, the cost of the opportunity, and the perspectives; then make a choice. But understand that you act without any guarantee of obtaining the expected and desired results.

Courage, perseverance, and faith give cohesion to success. To be successful, you must take control of your life, declare yourself responsible for your destiny, take advantage, and manage your freedom. Success also requires modification of lifestyle, willingness to compromise, and the ability to intermingle with and tolerate others who are different and have different viewpoints. You must be able to hear the truth, even when it shocks and hurts; you must be able to wait when some adjustments and changes are slower than expected. You need not only the will to succeed, but you also must make your will succeed.

Different groups must be aware of their projected images vis-à-vis the others—attitude, character, discipline, perseverance, dress code, and dedication to their emancipation. No one is going to hand you happiness and success on a silver platter. You must work for it and show that you deserve it. People judge you on the way you behave, the way you dress, the way you talk, the way you walk, the way you interact with others, the way you function socially, and your ability to deal with conflicts. The loudmouths with loud music, toxic vocabulary, and hostile and negative attitudes are consigned to their own place. They will not be admitted where they don't fit in. They would not like it there anyway. You must be permeable to necessary changes and adjustments without selling your soul. You are not called to give up your core beliefs and values, but you must be willing to make some adjustments. For example, someone is rightfully or wrongfully accused of murder. Imagine he shows up in court with his pants sagging way below his waist and a tee shirt that reads "I love to kill." How do you think this will influence the judge? Remember, even if justice must prevail, human beings can be biased and influenced by appearance.

Furthermore, your behavior may reflect badly on other people in your group. This can have a domino effect. A cow with a long tail cannot haphazardly jump over the fire; there is always the risk that her tail may be caught in the flame. By the same token you should not be a bunch of muscles with no spine, or like some liquid that takes the form of the container in which it is placed. You need equilibrium, a balance of common sense that can help you navigate to reach to the shore. You cannot function and succeed in a normal environment, while adopting a pathological behavior. When in Rome, do as the Romans do. In other words, do not make waves, do not make people feel threatened or uncomfortable when they are around you. This does not mean you have to be a lamb and let everyone take you to the abattoir. The antagonistic, paranoid approach will backfire. The docile, unconcerned, careless life will not help either. There are universal assets, essential characteristics that give the profile of those who are bound to succeed; and it crosses genders, races, creeds, beliefs, and sexual orientation. They include loyalty, courtesy, positive attitude, discipline, respect of established norms, reliability, perseverance, a sense of responsibility, generosity, altruism, compassion, teamwork, and the spirit of service. You need to have a spine and avoid sidesteps. You cannot make it when you seek refuge in the fortress of complaints, grudges, and isolation. Who wants to share the company of those who can only be negative and complain about everything under the sun? You must be able to endure the typhoon and tsunami of today to enjoy the sunny tomorrow.

When poverty and deprivation envelop you like a spider's web, only an extreme effort can free your mind from anger, blame, animosity, and jealousy and make you see beyond the present situation. Positive thoughts and the hope of a better tomorrow, along with appropriate actions, are like a breath of fresh air on a hot summer day, or like a fountain of cold water that suddenly appears in the middle of a dry and stormy desert. Remember, they can take away your physical freedom, but no one can imprison your mind or prevent you from nourishing positive ideas, no matter what the outside circumstances are. You must make a deliberate, conscientious decision not to let the outside things poison and intoxicate your thoughts, while taking steps to provoke changes. People who survive torture and privation make it because of their state of mind and their ability to care for others, despite their limited means.

Alas! How often success has been considered a utopia, a mirage, a hallucination for many! There are times when only a superhuman effort can help you float above your current situation to make you contemplate a gleam of hope at the other end of a dark tunnel. But you have to cherish that little gleam of hope. It is like the necessary spark that tends to grow and gain ground within your darkened heart and get the fire going. With the eyes of hope, you can already contemplate the result of determination, perseverance, and restraint that helps you to stay afloat. The circumstantial convulsions of the current situation can no longer affect you to the point of distracting you from your goals. Remember, great ideas alone do not guarantee success. You also need action, discipline, resources, and perseverance, along with appropriate policies in place.

A friend has a beautiful landscape. Every year, he spends a lot of time taking care of it. It is always filled with gorgeous flowers, fruits, and vegetables. One spring, he took ill and had some surgery that required bed rest for quite some time. Guess what happened to that beautiful garden. It was unrecognizable.

Any piece of land—no matter how fertile or beautiful— if it is left untended, is guaranteed to be covered with bramble and thorns. The weeds grow faster and need no special care. The same is true in everyone's life. If you leave your brain unoccupied, it becomes saturated with anger, hate, jealousy, frustration, discouragement, and all kinds of evil ideas and negative propaganda. The bottom line is that you must cultivate your gardens if you want to pick healthy and juicy fruits.

Doing nothing has never been and can never be an option for those who want to make it in life. Furthermore, if you keep on trying, yet you do not make it, nobody will really know. But if you stand idle, people will know and will talk about it. Just as on the battleground of war, in the battle for life, the key words are action and self-defense. Preserve your existence while looking out for your comrade and working toward peace, security, and stability. You may not always obtain the expected results, but you must continue to fight and never surrender. The key difference is often in the planning and the strategies to win and make a decent living. When the eyes are on the future and the goal, you can find the strength to struggle until you make it. Rain or shine, pain or joy, nothing can deter you from the triumph of your ideals. You must keep on moving forward; nothing else should distract you from your game plan.

If you are in the disadvantaged camp, you are playing on four fronts:

- Take stock of yourself; do your best to do the things that only you can do for yourself and for the betterment of your peers. Know yourself and appreciate the features that make you unique. Be proud of them!

- Be tactful and manage your relationship with others who are likely to facilitate the upward movement of your group, not necessarily because they genuinely want to but because it is a necessity for them.

- Expect misunderstanding and indifference from various sources, including your own people. Hope and work for the best, but be prepared to deal with the worst if it comes.

- Stay committed to change. Be involved in ways and means that can bring change in the community, the country and the society for fairness for all.

The revolution is first and foremost in the mind, where the need to strive is triggered, where the seeds of dreams are planted. What you see, read, hear, repeat, feel, and internalize will affect your decisions and their outcomes. You must develop the ability to filter the ideas that come from all sources, including people who mean well but who are not helpful to the cause. If you do not believe you can amount to anything good, then that is exactly what is going to happen. If you only share company with those who constantly call you names and tear you down, how can you be built up? There is no way to help someone who lets others convince him or convinces himself that he is just a good-for-nothing slob, an insignificant biped who is just walking around in misery until he drops.

Anything multiplied by zero is zero. When you are in a peculiar, difficult, disadvantageous condition, the first step toward any improvement is to take inventory of yourself, become aware that the current situation is bad, and make a personal, internal resolution to change. Change your thoughts, conceptions, visions, and behavior; and more often change your environment, at least mentally. You must stop comparing yourself with others in a negative way. You are a man! You are a woman! If anybody else can do it, so can you. No time to feed hatred, jealousy, frustration, envy, revolt, inferiority, and anger in to your system. You have wasted too much time with these kinds of feelings. It is catch-up time. All of these are toxic to you both physically and emotionally. When you are angry, you are unpleasant, rude, and scary. Who is going to want to help someone who is arrogant, foulmouthed, and even threatening? You have observed time and time again that people who are courteous and well-mannered get things done their way and manage to make people go out of their way to help them. Even those who are paid to help only do the minimum for people with a bad attitude. Instead of reacting with rage, you must act gracefully. If you must compare yourself with others, it must be only in order to build yourself up, to imitate the good qualities and personalities that can help to bolster your morale.

The knowledge and technology needed to succeed are not genetically infused. They have to come from others. But people will be more reticent to share if you rub them the wrong way. To put it bluntly, the winning attitude is always a nice and pleasant one.

You must objectively identify your shortcomings and take steps to eliminate them or reduce them to their minimum, while strengthening your good qualities.

Do not accumulate too many activities at once. It is better to concentrate your energy toward accomplishing one thing perfectly than to be all over the map with little concentration on each.

Try to finish the task you started before you venture into so many things at once.

Get rid of your inferiority or superiority complex, while remaining practical, and without being naïve. Show that you are mature and strong enough to take a few blows here and there. Of course, you will be kicked a lot in your life. If you give some you get some, but try to get less and give more.

Stay away from arrogance, complacency, and the spirit of self-sufficiency. Do not be overly sensitive. Know what you want and be willing to play the game to make it, as long as it is not against your values. Exploit your strong points to their maximum. The more assets you discover, the more tools you acquire; use them to catch up. Learn to use every single situation to your advantage. Use every occasion and opportunity to improve yourself: education, re-education, training sessions, and seminars.

Remember to prepare the future generation, discover your heritage, and work on your legacy.

Beware of neocolonialism that is meant to exploit your peers and your own people, who go through the same struggle with you. Do not sell them short just for you alone to get ahead at their expense.

Get rid of many obstacles like fear, anger, excuses, self- imposed limitations, negligence, laziness, mediocrity, and personal shortcomings that may accumulate to make you impossible, intolerable, unproductive, and uncorrectable. Know and obey the laws. No matter how successful you are, how popular you are, you can never be above the law. Some are even watching for your least peccadillo.

Identify those professional dream killers. They are there to rain on other people's parades and kill people's dreams, because they have none for themselves. Build up carefully your circle of influence. Keep pushing the frontiers of your attainable goals. Fight against the tendency toward selective amnesia. That is the tendency to forget those who helped you get where you are, or to be so ashamed of your past that you forget it altogether and want to forget anyone that was a part of that past. The past must be a springboard to propel you into the future. Past and present serve as solid foundations to build up the future. The key ingredients to build such a future include perseverance, discipline, integrity, respect, faith, courage, service, attitude, and gratitude. You must impose upon yourself some strict principles to be observed without any indulgence, without being trapped in a labyrinth. Never exchange a good quality of life for chasing extras that may not be a pressing need at that time. In other words, take time to enjoy every step of success. Never approve of abuse, injustice, or unfair treatment of your fellow man. And always use your time judiciously.

Regardless of the field, there is a common trait found in all professionals. It is their ability to finish their task, respect their commitment, and work and go the extra mile to make it happen. The naïve person, who is just observing superficially, may believe it is easy, but no qualified champions can take their work lightly; before they are qualified as champs, they must invest time to training themselves physically and mentally. After winning a contest, none of them goes back down to rest and do nothing else. No! They keep training and pushing themselves. All of them believe there is always room for improvement. Once you believe you have reached a plateau, you are no longer in the race and may as well give up the championship belt. You are in the arena for success for life. You identify your needs and the domain where improvement is needed. You make the necessary adjustments, you evaluate the results, and life goes on. The more you persevere, the easier the trend becomes. You identify ways and means to minimize your errors and exploit your advantages to reach your goals. There is no more room for vengeance, meanness, and immaturity. The more perilous and difficult the road, the more radiant is the victory. Give up selfishness, covetousness, and the tendency to blame others and look for excuses. Instead, press along and contribute to your own miracles. The key differences that make the scale tilt to your advantage are your positive attitude, your relentless effort and determination, your foresight, and your assiduousness.

This world provides no free ride. You have to pay to play. There is no exception. In summary, if you want to succeed, regardless of your race, here are ten basic principles that you should follow:

1. Have a dream and a set of goals.

2. Take advantage of every single opportunity that comes your way.

3. Be discrete and prudent, but vigilant, and allow no excuses.

4. Study the alternatives carefully; most of them may not take you where you want to be and you only go around once. Some choices may even hasten your ruin. Beware of the detours.

5. Take inventory of what you have. Be appreciative of who you are and educate yourself to do better.

6. Remember: no one owes you anything. So, be grateful and hold no grudges.

7. Do not confuse diligence with impulsiveness.

8. Never let an opportunity pass without giving a hand to a brother or a sister in need.

9. Remember you are only human. When you err, when you offend, ask for forgiveness and repair what is repairable.

10. Do not neglect your spirituality.

The Elderly and Success

The Enemy Within: Getting Old

Like a nail at the mercy of a hammer, so is mankind under the ax of time. In the blink of an eye, you catch yourself having used thirty, forty, fifty years of your existence. Here you are admitted to the class of middle age, soon to be promoted to the rank of senior citizen or people of "the third age" or even "fourth age" group. This is a polite way to tell you that you are living the last minutes of the game and the other team is winning and has the ball. Just yesterday, your vision was 20/20, the contour of your face was perfect. You were filled with energy, your muscles were strong and firm, your legs were agile, and your hair was thick and full. What happened? No one seems to know. Suddenly, everything has changed. You would like to protest, to sign a petition, or even go on strike against such unfairness; but your ego tells you to resist.

The hourglass of time is inexorable. Your physiological functions, your mental and intellectual faculties decline. Malaise and physical discomfort are settling in without an invitation. Everything has plotted against you. What a frightening experience to see yourself slipping and sliding away downhill, and there is no one there to give you a helping hand. Worst of all, you more or less know the ultimate outcome. The mist of uncertainty is taking charge, and from the first step you see the hideous specter of death coming boastfully toward you. There is nowhere to run. Heaven! Help! Regardless of what you say, deep inside everyone wants to live forever.

Becoming an elder requires a lot of strength to confront issues that do not necessarily have answers. For instance: Who are you? How did you come about? Where are you going? Why hasn't anyone come back to give you a quick preview on what to expect? It is as if you were kidnapped and placed on a train with lightning speed. You do not know where it is heading, and no one can stop it to let you off. You know the ultimate destination. You do not want to go there, but no one can help you. The organic modifications of getting old are unavoidable. What can you do in the meantime? You can hide yourself in a dark, cold, miserable, and dirty corner awaiting the fateful call, while mourning, murmuring, and crying. Or, after spending most of your life on the crutches of hope and optimism, you can borrow the stretcher of your memories of your past experiences and do an instant replay, with the satisfaction of having had your time under the sun.

Many take advantage of old age as a time to pull out from the drawers of their memory the various activities they engaged in but had no time to enjoy before: songs, poems, unfinished books, childhood games and foolishness, the adventures of adolescence, the missteps of our youthful indiscretions, and the worries of adulthood. It is time to reminiscence, to reconcile the books and close the accounts. When your memories are languishing, it is worth disturbing your agony by some tickling here and there. Is it the time to agonize over the bumps of your character, to moan over your failures or ruminate over your mistakes? Or should you instead be grateful for being spared sudden death, or even dementia, and enjoy every precious minute and every breath you take? It all depends. It is up to each and everyone. When the weight of the years takes away your physical strength and exchanges it for pain and cramps, should you also allow it to make you and everyone around you miserable? Or, should you still be proactive and decide to savor the taste of being alive? Again, this is a personal choice. The beating of your heart is being lost in the whirlwind of the past, the illusions of your remaining strength, and the uproar of a misfit surrounding.

Facing the uncertainty of tomorrow, the only thing that is certain is the present moment; and you ought to enjoy it and make it pleasant for everyone who comes in contact with you. No thing or person can prevent you from taking advantage of what you have and what is left for you, except you. There is also the art of aging without being a grumpy old person. You must manage to protect your soul and your mind from being eaten out by the virus called aging. Joy, gratitude, and enthusiasm are not exclusively attributed to youth. You can still remain green in your soul, your spirit, and your philosophy of life. To remain young until death, you need a youthful attitude. To make it, follow the examples of the young people. They are optimistic and sure of themselves. They have plans, they are curious, eager to learn, and adventurous. They remain active and they have a good sense of humor. If you match these qualities with your wisdom and a positive attitude, this is a perfect combination.

Several factors determine the authentic age of everyone. It does not necessarily coincide with the chronological age that the calendar imposes on you. You need to take into account your physical and moral condition, your potential, the status of your mental and intellectual faculties, and your ability to function in a specific domain. You are in many regards the author of the final outcome of your life. Getting old has its advantages, such as maturity, wisdom, experience, financial stability, respect, credentials, and status. If you cannot turn back the chronological clock, you must at least take advantage of your assets and exploit the circumstances, instead of giving up and rolling over to die. You need also to learn more about the new factors and new discoveries that are promising for eventual longevity.

The physical aspect of growing old

Elderly people tend to suffer from diffuse aches and pains. Their vision is reduced and they may suffer from cataracts, glaucoma, macular degeneration, or the aftermath of a stroke or surgery. Once you cross the fourth decade of your life, it is as if a big truck filled with all kinds of ailments is parked right in the middle of your road and is looking through you with its radioscopic eye to discover which part or organ in your body to attack first.

Fortunately, except for some hereditary, genetic, racial, and environmental factors, you are not condemned to fall sick or remain seriously ill until you die. There have been a lot of studies, research, and progress to make the quality of your life better than it was not too long ago. There are factors that you must identify and take steps to modify. For instance, a sedentary life, smoking, drinking, drugging, eating a lot of fried greasy foods, excessive salt and sugar intake, obesity, and chemical products are a few factors that are detrimental to your health and can affect the quality and the quantity of your life. If you want to live longer, you need also to see your doctor regularly. Stay away from polluted areas, be active, and have a balanced diet that includes plenty of vitamins and antioxidants.

Nowadays, there are several beauty products aimed at keeping the entire body beautiful. Even esthetic surgery is available. Many manifest their satisfaction with esthetic actions, such as laser, collagen, Botox, lymphatic drainage, and anti-aging massage. It is clear you should not be gullible and let people take advantage of you. You should make sure of the safety of the procedures as well as the qualifications and training of those who want to perform them. The main idea is to continue to feel young, to conserve your vigor, your energy, and your youth. Everything is guided from the mind.

Memory—tricking a beautiful mind

A physician specializing in neurology sees many patients who want to know whether or not they have Alzheimer's disease. Generally, the main concern of the patients and their families is about the patient's memory. Some will attest to a decrease of memory, while others deny it. Memory is the faculty that retains and remembers information, learned facts, and the experiences of the past. It includes the ability to remember events and retain the acquired knowledge and means to maneuver the facts already imprinted in your brain, which continue to influence the diagram of functioning in your daily life. It is an active process. Forgetting, in a sense, is a part of memory. There is a way to select and prioritize stored information to be retrieved when needed. With the accumulation of a lifetime of information, the mechanism must function flawlessly to avoid gridlock, panic, and confusion at the center of the thought process. Once the information is received, the process of fixation is triggered; it is recorded, stored, and retrievable upon command. After several decades, there is a gradual decline in your memory. It is generally imperceptible at the beginning. The brain is no longer the childhood sponge that absorbed whatever you saw, heard, thought, or read. As we get older, our brains become more selective to the various and constant bombardment of stimuli. Therefore, it is not terribly alarming if momentarily you forget one number of your bank account or the phone number of someone you have not spoken to for a while. Nevertheless, there comes a point when it can become pathological. For instance, if you are dealing with such situations as becoming disoriented in time and place, forgetting your age or birth date, or forgetting whether or not you had breakfast. When you cannot retain simple information for a few minutes or when mental calculations that you used to find simple become difficult to perform, you absolutely have to see a neurologist. The sooner you do it, the better.

Alzheimer's disease affects an appreciable percentage of people over sixty-five. The general early signs include loss of memory, reason, judgment, and language, to the point of interfering with the activities of daily life. Temporary delirium is not typically a disease on its own; it is rather the result of many symptoms that go along with a disease or a condition. This is why any mental change requires a visit to the doctor's office to find out why. The doctor will take the history, examine the patient, try to identify the possible physical and emotional causes, treat the treatable cause, and try to bring the patient back to the base of people in the same age and sex group. Getting old is a universal law; yet it is essential to see to it that you remain healthy in your entire body, including your brain.

The brain should not stay idle; it should always be stimulated. You should be eager to learn new techniques for doing old things and learning new things. "Use it or lose it" is especially true for the brain. Try to increase your vocabulary, learn new languages, read the newspaper and new books regularly. Do crossword puzzles and challenging games. Learn how to play a new instrument, how to sew or crochet, pay attention to whatever you did not do well in school or in life, and start improving in it. Attend classes in mathematics, calculus, statistics, drawing, painting, computers, gardening, etc. All of these can help the brain and the memory. Attend interesting conferences, do physical and mental exercises, imagine, think, describe, and visualize.

If you have illnesses, take the prescribed medications and be compliant. Sleep at regular hours. Avoid non-prescribed stimulants that can be detrimental. Here are a few steps that can help your memory:

- Before going to bed at night, prepare your calendar for the following day.

- When you wake up in the morning, try to remember what you wrote the night before.

- Use a notebook to write things down that need to be done.

- Be organized and disciplined. Put each thing in its proper place instead of having thousands of places to put one thing. Frequently rearranging a room or environment may make the elderly a bit confused.

- Avoid unnecessary changes that disrupt the visual image that helps locate things. Sometimes—if it is safe to do so—try to close your eyes and imagine the location of each object; ideally, your house should be so well organized that you should be able to find most of the things you need.

All in all, you cannot be passive. A well-balanced diet with little fat, a lot of antioxidants, physical exercise, mental, social, and spiritual activities could definitely help.

When you do your best, the rest does not depend on you. Avoid getting panicky and diagnosing yourself with diseases you may not have. When in doubt, check it out by going to see a qualified authority in that matter. Because of the aging process, the frustrations and the preoccupations, added to the side effects of some medications, the mind can lose its concentration. Much of the new information may not be retained because of lack of motivation and its position on your list of priorities. Get into the habit of doing one thing at a time; stay focused. Use some memory aids, such as calendars, labels, filing systems, folders, etc. Do not drop things here and there while the mind is floating in the clouds. Cultivate the good habit of making a mental note regarding what you do with everything. Just a note of caution: if you or your physicians reach the conclusion of Alzheimer's disease, regardless of the level, seek proper advice regarding giving the power of attorney to someone you can trust to manage your business. Later on, it will be difficult; and a few things may suffer while undergoing the process. Do not procrastinate.

Strangely enough, old people tend to have self-doubt regarding their ability to take care of their daily activities and their personal business transactions. This is possible. If you have convincing proof in that area, it is wise to seek help from someone you really know and who has proved himself to deserve your confidence. No one on this earth deserves complete, blind trust. It all depends on the subject matter, the time, and the circumstances. It is worth warning you about some predatory tactics, the use of all kinds of tricks to convince you that you are an invalid and to manipulate you into doing things that are not in your best interest.

Another avenue of concern for the elderly is their sexual performance. You and your partner should remain intimate as long as both of you are willing and you are physically able. Age is not a factor when it comes to deciding whether or not to have sex. But, as in many other areas, age, psychology, environment, and health affect sexual performance. The causes are multi-factorial. It is necessary to see your family physician to review your overall physical and psychological health status, and to make the appropriate recommendations including referrals to another specialist. Sometimes a vacation can be a good stimulant. Bear in mind that if you are in your late sixties and beyond, you should not put yourself in a race with a young person in his or her twenties. There should still be some ammunition ready to be used when needed.

Individual Development According to Erikson

Eric H. Erikson was a well known leader in the field of psychoanalysis and human development. Erikson, in his book Childhood and Society, skillfully described certain stages that every human being goes through. He proposed a theory of individual development that goes in stages: attention, anticipation, preparation, and self-control. Life is transitory. It is necessary to know how to adjust to time, identify shortcomings, and learn from the follies of youth and the trials of the past. We must be able to identify the signs that announce the coming of old age, be prepared to retire, and pass the baton to the next generation gracefully. That stage of life requires compassion and a spirit of altruism. It needs a personal, unbiased, and judicious inventory of one's life, which can sometimes be severe and unpleasant, but prevents the departure of loved ones. After we render our last breath, the main question will be: "What have we left for those who remain?" Is it heritage, financial resources, huge debt, insurance policies, a good or bad reputation? You must ask yourself what type of funeral you want. Where? How much does it cost? Can the family afford it? Who is going to take care of your surviving spouse, the children, and the other family members? Do you have a will? What will people remember you for? Did you put things in order? No one is too young to face these issues. Because no one can predict the future, it should be done promptly.

Erick H. Erikson—stages of development

1. Basic Trust Versus Basic Mistrust.

Drive and hope

This concept puts the emphasis on the durable impact of the quality of the relationship between the baby and the mother. After birth the child learns to depend on the mother, to find in her security and comfort. His life revolves around the mother's life. Even when the baby is not in his mother's arms, even when he does not see her close by his crib, he is still convinced of his mother's care. The type of relationship that the baby is able to develop with his parents and his surroundings provides enough confidence and allows him to develop love, confidence in himself, and confidence in his surroundings. Otherwise, he becomes anxious, distrustful, irritable, and depressed. In other words, the difference between the progress and regression of a child, between the integration and isolation of a child, is explained by the experiences the child had during the first years of his life.

THE ELDERLY AND SUCCESS

2.   Autonomy Versus Shame and Doubt.

Self-control and willpower

During the first years of life, the child learns to be secure and discovers the danger in his surroundings. He winds up knowing when to relax and when to defend himself, when to hold on and when to let go, when to satisfy his needs or not. Through time he becomes confident enough to develop a sense of autonomy. Everything is based on the experiences he had during those years. When the basic needs of a child are not properly satisfied, this will have an impact on the rest of his life. He will have to choose between hatred, suspicion, cowardice, love, confidence, and courage. He will be either shy and frustrated or confident and satisfied. These critical years will determine the life of that child. Therefore, the home, the school, the community, and the society play a key role in the future of the child.

3.   Initiative Versus Guilt.

Direction and purpose

During a child's development, he faces various challenges. He must develop ways and survival techniques. He has to develop strategies to survive. His curiosity leads him to adventures. He discovers that all of his dreams may not conform to the prescribed guidelines. He is not immune to danger. He will fail, he will get hurt, but he must learn. He does not always get along with his siblings. This is the moment of infantile sexuality, the incestuous complex mentioned by Freud: the castration complex or Oedipus complex. This is a challenging moment. The child will have to sort it out. Based on how it is handled, he will either become a well-balanced and responsible adult or a frustrated, anxious adult. Those childhood factors may affect his own children in his future life.

4. Industry Versus Inferiority.

Method and competence

As the child grows up, he is already a parent in training. He needs to acquire knowledge and skills. He learns to use the tools needed to have some assigned tasks done. He is exposed to reading, writing, manual works, etc. This allows him to develop a sense of responsibility. He develops his identity, broadens his horizons, expands his domain, and fertilizes his imagination.

5. Identity Versus Role Confusion.

Devotion and fidelity

With a well-balanced relationship to his environment, the child grows up to become a healthy adolescent. The transition is smooth. He continues to develop, to grow, and to meet new challenges. This is the time to define one's own identity; otherwise he becomes confused and uncertain about his future.

6. Intimacy Versus Isolation.

Affiliation and love

It is time to come out of the identity crisis. He knows who he is. He is willing and ready to contribute to his environment. He is ready to put into practice everything that he learned in the past, to begin friendships and intimate relationships, and to do his civic duties. He is willing to love and be loved. Otherwise, he may become distant, lonely, and isolated.

7. Generativity Versus Stagnation.

Production and care

Man is a human being who evolves, progresses, learns, and teaches. If children depend on adults, let us not forget that the elderly need the youth. The adults and the elderly should serve as instructors and guides to help the new generation to excel in productivity and creativity. Productivity is an essential step in the adequate development of the human being. If it fails, the person is likely to become an invalid.

8.   Ego Integrity Versus Despair.

Renunciation and wisdom

Man is a rational being who spends his life seeking and searching. It is necessary for him to find time to review his existence, analyze his actions, his relations with others, and consider his triumphs and his failures. This is the time to harvest the fruit of the first seven stages of his life. He is facing the eighth stage of his life: integrity of his ego or despair. In other words, it is time for the rooster to come home. He has to look into the mirror of his existence, evaluate his journey, and repair whatever can be repaired. At this juncture in life, if he has been consistent with himself and his principles, then he can sing with Edith Piaf, "I regret nothing!" He is ready to defend his legacy against any accusations. Every man is entitled to his form of integrity, based upon his culture, his civilization, his beliefs, his values, his ethics, and his knowledge. This integrity becomes the heritage of his soul, the seal of his moral paternity. When taking into consideration the various circumstances, he is to decide whether or not he is satisfied with his life. Then death loses its sting. Otherwise, he becomes agitated, desperate, irritable, miserable, and unbearable. With remorse and regrets, he sees death coming. He tries in vain to put it off. This despair is expressed as anguish and regret when he discovers that he has no more time left to repair the shortcomings that punctuated his life. It is too late to rewrite his story. It is too late even to write a new page, not even an addendum. It is time to play his role either as a hero or a subordinate. There is a close relationship between adult integrity and childhood confidence.

In summary, the last moment of one's life depends on the kind of existence lived throughout the stages of life. An elder who is well-balanced and confident represents the sum total of his entire life. It is a consequence, a harmonious whole that belongs to the total lifecycle on this planet. It is a required passageway to the other side. It cannot be left unprepared. With the recent prowess, so many things in life have become easy. Many people have the privilege to redo their physical beauty. Of course it is worth looking young all the time. But this does not make us escape reality: one day we will be gone. Have you made any preparation for what may come after? If not, where is your sense of priority?

Aging always comes too fast and death comes too early. The human's pilgrimage is like a flake of foam. We leave an incomplete life, like a bubble that bursts on the surface of the water. If death can come at any time, it does not dictate to us the quality of life that we should have before its visit. Why spend the rest of your life lamenting about death when you can enjoy every minute? When we were in our twenties, we had so much to do and so little time to do it. At seventy, eighty, or ninety, let us take time to enjoy every minute of our lives. This is the time to appreciate daily life, to delight in the smile of a child, listen to the birds singing, and contemplate the flowers and the butterflies, to be thankful for a meal, to appreciate the sun and the rain that fertilizes the land. Depending on your health and economic situation, you should take the time to travel, to visit here and there. After all, when we are old, what really matters is the quality of our life, the images we project upon our surroundings, and the legacy and heritage we pass on to the new generation and the ultimate destiny after death.

Practical advice for a rewarding and happy old age

- Live the various stages of life fully and enjoy the experiences of each stage. It is really pathetic to see an adult acting like a child.

- Learn early to define your goals and commit yourself to following them.

- Be a person of principles and live by them.

- Be useful to others. You will be glad to harvest the benefits later on.

- Take time to think and take inventory of your life. And make the proper adjustments when needed.

- Prepare others to continue your heritage when you are gone. Let your family know more or less what is going on, including your financial situation. Be candid.

- Make plans for your last days and prepare your funeral.

You might choose to die quietly in your bed after an accomplished life, with no regrets. Unfortunately, you do not have the privilege of deciding this. But there comes a time when you are more convinced than others that death is on its way. It is wise to take decisions regarding the end of your existence on this planet. Your wishes and decisions depend on your culture, your beliefs, the input of family members, the preferences given to the quality and the quantity of life, and the well-intentioned, professional advice of a competent physician. It is advantageous to plan early and to take an active part in all the final decisions as much as you possibly can, while you still have your lucidity. Some specific aspects of contemporary medicine require that we make clear decisions.

Depending on your decisions, some documents must be signed and notarized so that everyone knows your wishes. Bear in mind that other documents, such as your will, the money in the bank, and a report on your debtors and creditors, should be up to date. After you take care of everything, when the time comes to go, it will be sad. But those around you will have an inner peace because they know your death marks the end of all your suffering and worries. People will gather to celebrate the life of someone who preceded them on the road that we all must one day travel.

- Have at least an idea of what can happen to you after death.

You may be wrong, but be willing to learn before you come to a decision. This is very important: you have more or less lived your life, you have met many of your goals; you have built a reputation. You are definitely loved, respected, and appreciated. You have done your best! Or have you? What have you done in the spiritual domain? Why should that be left open to hazard? Let us do some reasoning. No intelligent man would leave himself vulnerable when he has a chance to protect himself. When you die unprepared or half prepared, here are the scenarios:

- If after death there is nothing else, you no longer know anything. Nothing is gained or lost.

- But if after death something else happens, shouldn't you get yourself ready for any eventuality? What if after death man is called upon to give an account of all his deeds? What will then happen to you? It is worth finding out more about what happens after death, now. After all, so many things have been said, shouldn't you at least be curious to know the different viewpoints?

- Take inventory of yours life, make peace with the supernatural. Sooner or later, each and every one of us must say good-bye. We do not know the date, but we know it is coming. Our lifestyle makes the difference when we are gone.

The Success of a Nation

The Enemy Within: Getting Old

We judge the success of a nation according to the standard of living of its citizens. An emancipated, well-educated, and stable population that has its basic needs met, a strong set of values, and a positive influence in the world at large inhabit a country that is successful. That is, we do not judge the success of a nation based on its weapons or its size, but rather according to its priorities, its choices, its actions within its limited resources, and its reaction in face of opportunities that come its way.

Individual success mirrors the condition of a nation. A society that does not take steps to foster the complete emancipation of everyone in it is condemned to fail. The main mission of every state is to provide security, stability, prosperity, and progress to its people. To reach such a goal, no sacrifice is too big, no price is too high, and no stone should remain unturned.

The country must provide the ideal environment where every citizen feels secure enough to shoot for the maximum of his potential. Of course, topography, people's various needs, the types and amount of resources, the projected common goals, and its political, social, and economic philosophy must be taken into consideration. The country must also clearly state the national objectives and priorities, while taking into account its moral values and its socioeconomic agenda. It needs to classify the different services available, what other services are needed, and how to improve the current system, while developing a dynamic interrelation among the different branches and levels of government. The relationship between the population and those in charge, between that nation and others, and the way it is perceived by other nations and leaders must not be ignored either. Those in charge must come up with a strategy, a set of policies that encourage creativity, ingenuity, pragmatism, prudence, and the perfection of individual talents and skills.

It is clear that globalization, the in-your-face, ever-present, biased media, and constant technological progress tend to make it more difficult for some leaders. The live coverage of every event in the world may bring along many challenges for some nations and may even cause the transformation of its physiognomy. The era of instantaneous cultural intercommunication imposes a change in people's manners, viewpoints, visions, and moral values. That metastatic process, once set in motion, may become an uncontrollable movement with an unforeseen impact on a small nation. Some people keep making the same mistakes by wanting to impose their own values, goals, and visions on the world. If they happen to carry enough political and economic weight, their views pass as the best views. This is a naïve approach to lasting peace. When you put a gun to someone's head, how much choice does he have? Arrogance and dictatorship are not the best ways to convince others of your democracy or your liberty.

Many actions neutralize their intentions and run the risk of causing just the opposite of what you want to achieve. Worse yet, this may last long after you are no longer on the political scene. The apparent success of a political misstep may mean it takes decades, even centuries to reveal the negative impact on the destiny of a given action. Freedom is not for sale. It is a way of life. Once you taste it, you do not want to go back to the old way of doing things. Those who act in good faith want to taste it for themselves. Nevertheless, there is no universal freedom. Each country may have its variation of liberty. What may be ideal for your own country may be detrimental for another. No one should suddenly decide to change another nation's culture through gunboat diplomacy. When you try to impose your culture and your way of life on another country, you are saying that yours is the best. How many will genuinely accept such a drastic trade? The best way to positively influence another nation is through examples, incentives, and respect.

Respect may in many cultures be more important than anything else. It is clear that change is the only real constant in life. However, to impose it on or implant it in another country is as easy as trying to teach an ant how to sing. It depends on the leader, the perception others have of him, his relations with his people, what is at stake, the condition of the opposing parties, and the fight within the group to exert the most influence. A synergic relationship among all the citizens and their leaders becomes an important asset for the nation's success. The progress of a nation requires the involvement of every citizen and every institution. The key is to find a way to appreciate the skills and competency of a nation without spoiling it, to stimulate it without bursting it.

Let Us Question History

To better apprehend the acuity of the various obstacles that every modern nation must face, open a window on the past. Review some data and gather the appropriate information of the given people in the past. The current world's achievements did not come overnight. The era of great discoveries was not built out of nothing. This is a continuous process built upon the past performance of our ancestors. The prehistoric societies had their challenges. They had to find ways to overcome the changes and inclemency of Mother Nature, as well as manmade threats, to survive. Because of a lack of transportation and communication, quite a few inventions might have been duplicated in different parts of the world. The archeologists, ethnologists, anthropologists, and sociologists have done their best to reveal the hidden treasures of the past.

The world system of every era depended on the strength and the central ability of each empire to control and expand its influence and the duration of its conquests. Each time a new empire emerges, it has the inherent duty to exploit the acquisitions of the previous empire and see to it that it does better, with greater prowess, to meet the new challenges. All empires were not equally powerful. The Babylonian, Assyrian, Greek, Mede (Persian), and Roman empires managed to really dominate their respective periods; yet they did not completely crush all kinds of peripheral pockets of antagonism. Many periods were known for their constant unrest and everlasting fights for supremacy, where each nation tried to gain preeminence over the others.

Despite all these fights, most of the great innovations and discoveries in the past were able to reach all the way to us in this century. They include the pyramids, the castles, monuments, palaces, temples, and various others architectural developments, migration, commerce, means of transport, and communication. They can serve at least as inspirations for our new and sophisticated conquests and achievements. Since then, the world has been known for its intellectual advancements in the arts and sciences during the industrial revolution; the refinement of manners, the abolishment of servitude, women's emancipation; the technical and industrial successes that started in the nineteenth century in electronics, medicine, communication, and aeronautics. And of course the latest inventions, such as the Internet, have put us on a brand new odyssey toward unlimited achievements in various domains, including leisure, comfort, economy, finances, education, health, travel, etc, on the World Wide Web.

Theoretically, everything has become instantaneously accessible to all. From the prehistoric era to the postmodern phase, our planet has known unimaginable and unpredictable successes. Human beings continue to outperform themselves. A quick consideration of the situation leads us to believe that the accomplishments are not evenly distributed. The great discoveries, a great number of scientists and those who receive the Nobel Prize, seem to come from one part of the globe. Why? There are a few key factors that seem to play a major role in the success of a nation. They are:

- A Cartesian approach where nothing is taboo, everything is put under scrutiny. Fanaticism should be avoided to give room to reason and logic.

- Prioritization of a nation's objectives.

- A nation's knowledge of its assets, its strengths, and its weaknesses. What can the citizens do? What do they need? What do they lack? Where can help be found to face the deficiencies?

- An environment where all the citizens are motivated to do their best for the success of their country and the success of humanity. This requires freedom to think, to question without any risk of being suspected by the state or the clergy. The citizens must be able to exploit their curiosity and conceive a better or a new way of doing things, to answer to new challenges in every domain.

- Freedom from all kinds of discrimination: racial, class, age, sex, etc. The country must be objective and act with probity and equity.

- Elimination of any system that condones division, antagonism of sectors, classes, and groups at the expense of the nation. It is shameful and inhuman for people of the same race, from the same country, with the same blood coursing though their bodies to go about killing each other for reasons such as ethnic or tribal cleansing, or religious beliefs or political affiliation. It is as if people went back to the barbarian era while in the twenty-first century. How can you explain this killing, suffering, and destruction inflicted on others in the name of ethnic appurtenance, political ideations, or religious beliefs? What value do we give to a human life, a life that we can take but we can never give back, that at the same time such a reprehensible act does not prevent us from facing the various challenges of life and our own death?

- A stable political system where each citizen feels he has his role to play. He can cherish his sense of belonging, of being significant and useful in his society. He must be convinced he is not dealing with a bunch of opportunistic pariahs who promise the moon and the universe but cannot provide the bare minimum. Instead, they are all out to get rich at the expense of the nation. He must evolve in a political system that does not clip his wings to prevent him from reaching his full potential, and making the difference in his life and the life of others. He needs a place where no one is above the law, where opportunities are available for all, where everyone does the best in everything he does. People want to see qualified people in appropriate jobs and proper pay for proper jobs.

For example, can you imagine a nation where only the poor pay taxes and utility bills, while the rich and those in the government, who get better pay than the poor, never pay a dime? Show me a country where the rich exploit the poor and transfer all the money to a foreign bank, and you have a country condemned to stay in disarray and poverty. Show me a country where the president, once elected, must spend most of his term fighting against inevitable coups d'état, and I will tell you that country is condemned to an everlasting new beginning. A country where the president and his executive staff consider themselves above the law is on its way to everlasting bankruptcy. A country that does not respect its heritage, where the intellectuals feel threatened, where everyone wants to do as he pleases is headed towards anarchy and disaster. Show me a country where the people are always exploited, frustrated, scared, mistreated, and you have a country without any future. Show me a country wrapped in its flag, frozen in its glorious past, lost in the clouds of its ancestors, but without any plan for the present and the future, and you have a nation without a present or a future.

A nation's success does not necessarily depend on its share of oil or diamonds. Otherwise, all the citizens from the countries rich in petroleum and diamonds would be prosperous. A developing nation must share a strong desire to take advantage of every situation and learn from every other country, including its so-called enemies. A constructive dialogue is always worthier than war and hatred. A mature nation must make sure it elects mature people at the helm of the government. It has no time for childish quarrels, nurturing divisive issues, and approaches that are sterile and static. It has no place for leaders who only pay lip service to the vital interests of the nation through spin and talking points but no real substance. A myopic vision prevents you from expanding, and it also isolates you. To succeed, you need the help of everyone; and you must learn how to deal with every other nation, respecting its cultures, beliefs, and ways of doing things. The only thing not acceptable is to betray patriotic pride, to misuse the power given, and to become a threat to people's lives.

Whether you like it or not, there is one world system nowadays. The United States of America has the ball. The Group of Eight is playing the main game and the United States is the captain of the team. The pragmatic approach is not to hate and resist but to find the best way, any possible alliance, to benefit your country. It is unfortunate to see so many nations engage in vain political rhetoric to bolster the egos of their citizens, while the populations are dying of hunger because of personal pride. A government that chooses to starve its people to death while pursuing weapons of mass destruction should be put on trial for high treason by its people, because it does not know its priorities.

A nation's success is not the business of a small group. It requires the engagement of everyone inside and outside of the country. There is no more room for those who would rather kill the dream than die for the dream. The cause of a nation must be greater than one man's little ego. There is no more room for parasites, or those who can only consume but cannot produce. This brings into place the immortal quote from John Fitzgerald Kennedy: "Ask not what your country can do for you; ask what you can do for your country." Too many people want to ascend to the main seat for the wrong reasons. A nation that requires well-deserved aid must also show others it is mature enough to handle its internal affairs as responsible people. If you are constantly fighting amongst yourselves like dogs and cats, if you keep making permanent enemies by holding grudges and being wicked and vengeful, the country ultimately will suffer. If your behavior is so childish that you need other nations to come in to keep you from constantly being at each other's throats, then how can you claim to be free and independent? Maturity must be demonstrated, not bragged about.

The Global Dilemmas of the Millennium

This postindustrial era remains favorable to a capitalistic society that is dynamic and requires frequent changes and adjustments in various domains. Ideally, capitalism works best in a democratic, secure, and stable society. At the heart of capitalism lies the concept of a market economy that is driven by supply and demand. The various enterprises aim at reaping the maximum profit at the lowest cost. However, to paraphrase Tocqueville, market and democracy can destroy civilizations. Some advocate social, national, and global transformations. Globalization has reached a point of no return according to many experts. Yet it is not without its problems, such as its impact on the environment, specific cultures, politics, the inequalities between the North and the South, lowering of wages, and economic insecurity. We are living in an interdependent world, yet it remains multipolar. A simplistic approach based on an old-fashioned one-size-fits-all theory is bound to fail.

There are different viewpoints advocating different approaches. On the one hand, there are the conservatives, who have run the show for years. They have a lot at stake, resist all signs of change, and want to keep the values within a certain order of priorities. On the other hand, the adventurers, who are excited for change, want to get rid of all barriers that may hamper the needed changes. For one group change is threatening, for another it is a welcome opportunity that is long overdue and is a generator of further robust performances. The whole civilization is at a critical crossroads. What is more frightening is that no one can remain in the intersection. To stay neutral risks being overrun by events. Some people are even talking about a crisis due to a generation gap, a disconnect. The new generation must take over. The hope is that at least it remembers what it was taught by the older generation.

The world situation is changing, with challenges from all directions. Globalization, led by the United States, its allies, and a coalition of people of goodwill from everywhere can ultimately overcome those hard times and maintain world peace, security, justice, and stability for all. Everything must be geared toward the well-being of every citizen of the planet. Europe and the United States must not antagonize each other, but cooperate for the common good. One of the key reasons the western world is successful is its firm belief in democracy and freedom for all. It must add to this a uniform conduct and not change the rules according to the perceived adversary. Democracy, security, stability, justice, and discipline form the cornerstone for any durable plan for the progress of humanity. The emphasis should be less on being conservative or liberal, being from the right or the left, being Democrats or Republicans with a socialistic or capitalistic approach, but more on the common goals for the common good. Name-calling tends to alienate and create a divide. The only name that is significant is that we are humans living on a planet full of all kinds of challenges. All are involved in the business of surviving. You must be united to face the problems from a multipolar world. The formula would wind up with a mega-nation, an "estate world" aimed at developing an ideal system where everyone can reach the maximum of his potential, where the lazy ones, the pariahs, and criminals, are found and dealt with appropriately, where the weak, the homeless, and the underserved all have opportunities—based on qualifications and motivation— to emerge with dignity.

How To Solve These Problems

Realize such a challenge concerns us all (there is no free ride). Rank challenges by priority (not necessarily in the following order):

- Ability to respond immediately to any catastrophe, anywhere, and at any time.

- Necessity to be united in the fight against terrorism in all its forms and to stop any kind of proliferation of weapons of mass destruction.

- Eradication of diseases, elimination of poverty, and promotion of technical and scientific economic expansion throughout the world.

- Opposition to racism, genocide, crime, and drug smuggling.

- Protection of the environment and awareness of global warming, as well as quantity and quality of potable water.

- Democratic promotion of freedom; showing the advantages of democracy through example, not by shoving it down anyone's throat; cessation of support for any despotic, corrupt, and totalitarian system.

- A macroeconomic, macro-sociologic, and anthropologic view of the world that permits special attention to be given to resolve the problems of inequality of resources, education, science, moral values, culture, way of life, and the best functioning system for every individual population.

- Prevention and preparation of all emergency scenarios, including natural disasters, terrorism, etc. Develop the ability to get along together to solve them and deal with them conjointly.

- Special attention paid to the younger generation so as to have a global impact on their education, religion, teachings, beliefs, motivation, etc.

No one should have to fight all the current challenges and those to come alone. It would be such an ideal situation to see Marx, Keynes, Tocqueville, and Greenspan sitting together and sharing their economic philosophy. The Unites States will continue to navigate as leaders with less turbulence and furious waves, if it shows more diplomacy, tunes down the rhetoric, and masters the use of its politics of carrot and stick. People will keep their eyes on the carrot if they know it is real and fair.

Dialogue, sympathy, and empathy should not be put aside. Weapons alone cannot solve the world's problems. When reason and prudence are ignored to the profit of arms and harsh rhetoric, all bets are off, especially when you have so many young people in a good part of the world who are dissatisfied and feel alienated from the mainstream. Some of them are financially stable. It is worth investigating. Communication and education must get some priority. Everyone has dreams and would like to be able to fulfill them. The United States and Europe must be tactful enough so that those they help do not feel they are treated like slaves or beggars. The allies must play their role and honor their engagements. Any antagonistic approach must disappear and leave room for cooperation. There is too much to lose in fostering cleavage among nations at this stage of the game. The world is facing sociocultural, ideological, religious, moral, ethnic, and ethical crises. This is the time for world community, a great federation in which every state, every nation maintains its dignity and its identity while moving along toward a better world, toward unity and diversity, in which all the people work together to improve the condition of every human being; where security, defense of fundamental and social human rights, the protection of the environment, peace, prosperity, equity, and justice should have precedence over any little personal discord.

Strength stems from the chains formed by a world united to overcome the different challenges. Every nation should count and should have its role to play, based on its resources, its economic weight, and its demographic pole. It is time for a planetary geopolitics, a global economy that sees to it that all people are secure, stable, and motivated to contribute their fair share.

There should not be any parasitic nation that is there only to be fed and taken care of. There must be a well-balanced system with the appropriate structures to verify, implement, and correct the machinery. The fall of the Iron Curtain can teach us valuable lessons. Wouldn't it be great to have a definite date to wipe out famine from the globe, for instance? Or immunize all children against certain prevalent diseases that destroy so many babies? Or teach the world's population how to read and write? To reach such noble goals, there must be a global system that is equitable, transparent, and diligent.

Desires and Rights of All People

- Food, clothing, and lodging.

- Health, security, and stability.

- Basic education in science, art, literature, and technology.

- Civic and moral instruction.

- Electoral modalities free of threats and constraints.

- Administrative relations; harmonious military, judicial, and financial cooperation.

- Adequate work, leisure, and comfort.

- Comparable roles for men and women in social, religious, political, governmental, and financial domains.

- Adjustment of scientific techniques and abilities to a level that is globally competitive.

- Competitive standing in children's health, preventive medicine, prevention and protection against abuses such as domestic violence, children's slavery, and forced labor.

Obviously, this is not a complete list and it should be adjusted according to the given population and its priorities. The main idea is to identify the needs of the nation and to take concrete steps toward satisfying them. No nation will succeed in isolation, inertia, empty rhetoric, propaganda, and false accusations, or in attacking another nation. Instead, it should develop a selective permeability to learn and extract what is best and what is susceptible to work for its people. The main idea is to cause the betterment of every citizen of its nation. This is a gigantic task, and it must start with the head of the nation.

The leader of the nation cannot be a flaky stripling, a self-proclaimed whippersnapper who lives by creating controversy, who feeds on propaganda, empty promises, or immature incompetence. If one citizen cannot eat, the leader should not be eating either. If one citizen has no place to sleep, neither should the leader. He should in fact have nightmares until he solves these problems. If one citizen is naked, how can the leader have countless wardrobes? If the people in the streets are poor, hungry, and sick, the leader should be the first poor man to fight for them all. If one child is sick and cannot go to school, how can the leader's children be well and go to the best schools in the country? The nation's leader is the father of all the children in the country. The leader shares the suffering, the pain, the joy, the success, the defeat, or the humiliation of any citizen.

I still remember many instances from my childhood where there was nothing or almost nothing to put in our mouths. Regardless of the situation, whatever she found, my mother would always make sure all of us had something before she took what was left. One day

I asked her why she always did that. She replied, "You must live, even through my death." The authentic head of state should not back down in front of any sacrifices to further the cause of his country. He should always do what is best for the nation, not be stuck with ideas that are detrimental to his nation. He should be willing to move heaven and earth to see to it that his people have access to the minimum: food, hygiene, potable water, a place to sleep, clothes to wear. Then he should take steps for employment, education, health, and quality and length of life. He should communicate regularly with his people. This means he should find efficacious ways and means to understand, interpret, express, and listen to the various messages and exchanges through words, gestures, body language, and the various media, including a steadfast stern silence. The moral tone of a leader is reflected upon the nation.

Authentic Leader

Leadership is the ability to influence others directly by showing them the way or telling them what to do or how to behave. It is a position of command. The leader happens to master the art of directing and influencing the crowd. He is in front and orients people. He is usually the most visible and the main target; others follow him. In the postmodern era, his obligations also include pacification, organization, and coordination, controlling and reaching specific set goals. He must motivate and influence his supporters to make it to where he wants to go. In other words, the leader takes necessary steps and commits some acts that embody different functions and domains to reach his objectives.

Ten qualities of an authentic leader

The true leader distinguishes himself or herself by the following qualities:

1. The capacity to lead others, motivate them, communicate goals to them, and to inspire them through words and deeds (honesty, behavior, fairness, incorruptibility).

2. The disposition and the responsibility to work with others (assimilation to the group, common goals).

3. The capacity to withstand challenges and introspection.

4. The stern will to listen and maintain an open mind to advise as well as to criticize.

5. The desire to accept responsibilities, to risk and even to lose advantages for the sake of the cause.

6. A dynamic approach and an open spirit when considering each problem.

7. Ability to master the art of communicating the true vision with a passion.

8. The ability to serve as an example of courage, moral values, and professional ethics.

9. The capacity to manage various sources of pressure with tact, calm, and moral stability.

10. The ability to submit to a higher authority.

Administrative assets

The authentic leader is also a skillful administrator who can:

*   Understand the complexity of human beings and adopt a philosophy that takes into account the susceptibility and weakness of everyone.

- Understand the different influences on the behavior and the reaction of each human: nationality; level and type of education; culture; fundamental beliefs; and social, economical, educational, religious, and political forces.

- Be familiar with the community, its strengths and weaknesses (education, economic power, and political connections).

- Identify and master the necessary rules to develop and maintain good relations with others.

- Strengthen the intellectual background through education, advanced studies, or the pursuit of personal objectives.

The authentic leader must know how to:

- Remain focused on the main lines of a project while delegating the minor details to the qualified cooperators.

- Delegate certain tasks to the staff with specific instructions, without the absolute necessity for daily personal involvement to make it through.

- Listen to the questioning, concerns, worries, hesitations, doubts of others and be able to inspire confidence and bring the appropriate adjustments. Respect others' opinions.

- Make decisions according to the objectives, the facts gathered, and the circumstances, without prejudging.

- Congratulate and encourage those who are devoted, and correct mistakes with dignity and respect.

- Respect the experts and beware of their limitations.

- Prepare plan A, plan B, and even a plan C for every project.

- Be aware of everything that must be performed in order for a project to be successful, even in times of severe adversities.

Handicaps to a leader's success

If there is such a thing as destiny, then character is likely the determining factor. Character and the different attitudes of a leader can hamper his ability to lead a group or his people. Features such as selfishness, malice, arrogance, mood swings, cynicism, self-sufficiency, obsession, and indecisiveness, fear of failure, laziness, amateurism, intemperance, and lack of self-control will affect the success of the leader.

The risks of a leader

Whether you are judged as great or below average, as a leader you will face undesirable situations and have to make decisions that are unpopular. The journey of the leader includes ascension to leadership, incomprehension, persecution, privation, accusations, aversion, rejection, and ultimate chastisement.

Ascension

Generally, as a group or a nation is going through some difficult time, people are looking for a way out. In the midst of panic and chaos, and for some unclear and nonspecific reason, you rise to the occasion and start uniting people around you; you are giving them hope and proposing viable solutions. You are propelled to the top to handle some difficult situations. People like you and want to support you, and they honor you for your courage and charisma and sacrifices for the common cause. Soon you also will discover that you have enemies you never met who want you to fail by any means available to them. You must stay the course and be yourself. Remain the leader of everyone. Provide help and service to all. Be as determined to help your foes as you are your friends. Do not be ashamed of your past. Do not forget where you come from. Be careful while you are in your current situation, while working for a brighter future for all.

Incomprehension

The leadership task in itself is irksome. See to it that your associates or assistants, from the beginning, know your goals. Let them know where you stand, what you want to be done, how, and for how long.

Nevertheless, you are going to be pulled in many directions. Everyone's project is the most important and they all want undivided attention and privileges. This leads to tense moments of misunderstanding and even false accusations. Learn not to take them personally. Prioritize your interventions. Learn early to master ways for effective communications. Be sincere, truthful, and genuine. Let them know what you want; and when change comes, let them know why you change as soon as you discover you need to adjust. Do not be at the mercy of the different winds of opinions. Do not base your actions on the polls taken from the population. Yet, do not be blind, arrogant, and self-righteous. If you make mistakes, admit them, take steps to avoid any more faux pas, and then move on.

Persecution

Do not expect to be everyone's idol. Some people will never be happy unless they can be ranked in the camp of the opposition. Generally, around two-thirds of those placed under your leadership will accept you, love you, and want you to succeed despite your flaws and your shortcomings. The remaining third will be in the opposite camp. So instead of being irritable, angry, and obsessed by a few people, take the situation as normal and do the best you can to remain the leader of everyone. Besides, there are instances when the opposition can help you and keep you as vigilant as possible. The different opinions may show you some weakness that needs to be taken care of. Often, only the opposition will point out those gaps. It is worth noting that some people will always be on the opposing side. They may cause harm or paralysis, trigger panic, or even make plans for homicidal acts. This is why you need to be vigilant without being paranoid. Allow anyone the privilege and the courtesy to be heard. Try to understand their viewpoints and where they are coming from. If they are right, do not be stubborn or too proud to make appropriate changes when changes can improve the situation. The authentic leader always allows a dialogue.

Do not waste your energy fighting or trying to destroy all your enemies. You can try to win them through your calm, your fairness, your dignity, conduct, and ethics. Do not antagonize them in public. Many times, it is worth providing what is needed instead of what is deserved. When you are gone, they may remember you and even wish you would come back. Ignore their sarcasm, the caricatures, and the virulent attacks. They may be very hard to take at the moment, but they are able to mold you into a better servant for the common cause. Who knows? When reminiscing tomorrow, this may even provoke a good laugh.

Privation

Often sooner rather than later, the leader discovers that his function puts him in an isolated spot. It is lonely up there. There are secrets that are confidential that you must keep within you until you are six feet under. Certain worries and apprehensions must stay within you, and no one can hear them. The good leader learns to succeed with the means available, even if he has very limited resources. There are but few administrations that provide all the leader needs to perform his duties. To the contrary, the leader often seeks to provide, to cater to the needs of the administration and of those under him. The leader must learn how to manage, even from nothing, in order to make it. Genial acrobatics will cover many things that are lacking. Learn to recycle. Be creative in reorganizing and reusing the materials available. If you do so, those who are trying so hard to clip your wings, embarrass you, or boycott you will be surprised. The leader must learn how to live in a mansion or in a dungeon.

Accusations

Do not think you are immune to the most sordid or repugnant accusations from false witnesses. The leader is always the first one to be blamed when things go wrong, and the last one to be praised when things are okay. People tend to read into every little insignificant word or action. They will lend you intentions that never crossed your mind. Every move you make and every deed is placed under close scrutiny. The worst part is that there are rumors and accusations that only time and history can disprove, sometimes many generations after your death. You should have only one concern: be sure you are at peace with yourself. Have a clear conscience. Do what you believe and believe in what you do. God knows and sees everything. He is the ultimate judge. Stay away from questionable appearances, doubtful and compromising situations. The accusations are unfortunate. They can derail the course of a leader. Make sure they are false. Then they will make you a stronger and better person.

Aversion

The leader should be pragmatic. Those who applaud you today may be the same people to reject you and seek your head tomorrow, and vice versa. The true leader is not seeking recognition. You are not craving love nor destroyed by hatred. Your only burden is to serve the cause to the best of your abilities. You work to fulfill your engagement and further the cause. You cannot operate at the mercy of public opinion. Negative sentiments and emotions must not condition your actions or reactions. You must avoid allies too close to the administration, who have a fanatical approach to your plans and deem that whatever you come up with is pure gospel. Those zealots may have to pay a high price when you are no longer around. Love begets love. Hatred begets hatred. Be careful. Do not succumb to your impulses to vengeance. Again, be the leader of everyone, but never be the private property of a small group or some special interest groups.

The ultimate price to pay

History tends to repeat itself. The facts are there to prove it. Today you are famous, popular, and well-liked. You are the idol of the nation; tomorrow you are a disgrace. This is why you need to be consistent. Do not let any praise get into your head and make you take yourself too seriously, to the point of believing you are a god. You are not! Enjoy the moment while you are under the spotlight. But be considerate and humble. There are countless ways to eliminate a leader, ruin his reputation, and push the people he has been defending to revolt against him. It goes with the territory. The greatest leader that humanity has ever known, He whose business it was to take care of the people in many ways, had crucifixion as His ultimate reward. You are convinced of your leadership when you lead without any hidden agenda and when you love the cause without expecting anything in return. Curiously enough, the best way to prove it is to be willing to die for that same cause. Jesus Christ said, "The good shepherd gives his life for the sheep"

The leader of a nation

With the current prevailing climate in this world, it only takes an idea, a few hundred or thousand dollars, and a willingness to work hard to make it in this world. Western history has countless examples of simple men who became top successes according to the criteria of the world. Nevertheless, what is expected for someone to be elevated to the helm of a nation goes beyond what is required for the common man. A nation's leader has to deal with many factors. His success depends on a variety of scenarios, including a symbiotic reaction between natural and supernatural facts. In general, the leader may engage in many activities, counting on his own assets, his approaches, his strategies, but he also has to face circumstances and cases that are overwhelming.

There are challenges that come to wipe you out like a furious wave when you least expect it. Even if you are not religious, many times you will need to call upon a supernatural being. A quick look at the Nazarene, Jesus Christ, will help you to elucidate a few of His qualities that made Him such a great success. Even in a historical perspective, He was a leader. He distinguished Himself through His gentle, affable, humble, positive, spiritual, loving, convincing, charismatic, responsible, persevering, respectful, sympathetic, altruistic, understanding, serving, flexible, and benevolent character. He was well aware of the scope of His mission. He showed skills and special talents to distinguish Himself. He exhibited features that all leaders should imitate. They include:

- An unfailing, unselfish love to serve.
- The charisma to attract the crowd.
- The example of courage, generosity, and motivation
- Concentration on the goal.
- The sense of planning, a way of communicating the vision, and delegation of power to execute what is already decided.
- A way of encouraging and congratulating others for their work done.
- Acknowledgement of boundaries.
- The ability to be firm, yet tactful, fair, and plain.
- The ability to listen and to cooperate.
- Self-sacrifice for the cause.

The strategies of a leader

The true leader knows his weaknesses and his strengths. He does his best to acquire the necessary knowledge to fill in gaps in his domain as much as is possible. He shows a practical approach and a discerning spirit. He is a person of action. Considerate, he knows how to comfort, congratulate, or reprimand without embarrassing others. He projects the image of being the servant to all. He has no hidden agenda. He is not manipulative. His interests are confounded with those of the people he serves. He is neither the master nor dominator, far less a god.

The style of a leader

Some people are born leaders but they can become politicians. Every natural leader has an approach and a style of leadership that makes him who he is. Sometimes he is not clearly conscious of a specific style that he is using. The fact is that others who observe him may try to catalog him in one category versus another. The factors that contribute to making him who he is include character, genes, temperament, personality, education, environment, family, his viewpoint, attitude, beliefs, and culture. When taking these factors into consideration, leadership style falls into the following categories:

Autocratic

Those who dictate and control everything.

Democratic

Those who take into consideration the equal rights and views of those involved in a given situation.

Participative

Those who lead with a team approach where everyone participates plainly.

Consultative

Those who love to consult others, seeking their opinions and advice.

Debonair

Those who love to please everyone and seem to give everybody the green light to decide and do it all.

In reality, many leaders show a combination of all of the above, based on the time, the issues, and the circumstances. The mature leader must adjust as needed in order to succeed.

Regardless of the chosen style, the authentic leader is wise and bright enough to make the necessary adjustments in a given set of circumstances and at the opportune moment. The appropriate style is not carved in stone, nor is it sustained by the law of the Medes and Persians. Every group, every community, every society, every nation requires more or less a general basic approach, according to the values, protocol, and culture, as well as enough insight to adjust and cooperate for a given peculiar situation. Special occasions and special situations require special attention. The fundamental steps remain basically as follows:

1. Identify the objectives. Define them clearly. Determine their feasibility. For example, it is known that education in various domains tears down the curtains of ignorance and fosters a socioeconomic emancipation of the people. You need not only talk about it, but be specific. Develop a strategy to educate all the people at a given time. Set parameters to measure progress and make the necessary adjustments to meet such a challenge right on target.

2. Get organized to reach the goals in a reasonable period, with ways to measure the progress made (inventory of resources, availability, and use).

3. Distribute the load of responsibilities by giving to everyone according to his ability and his motivation to participate where he can excel. Delegate the necessary authority to get the job done.

4. Be able to review, get reports, and make appropriate adjustments.

5. Be able to lead through example. You, your family members, and the members of your cabinet should be the first to conform to the rules and obey the law of the land.

Epilog

Congratulations! You have come to the end of the long and challenging odyssey about a successful life. Certain parts of this book need to be read more than once; certain ideas and key words have to be underlined or even memorized. Now, some pertinent questions need to be addressed: What are you going to do with the information covered? What steps have you taken to put into practice what you have learned or what you were reminded of? You must not put it off anymore. Now is the time to start. First, find yourself some time alone and think about your life. Get a pencil and paper and start writing. Make it a habit to walk around with a pencil and paper, or whatever is convenient for you. Nothing should be left to chance. One step at a time and you are on your way to overcome the devil of procrastination.

Remember, this book—like many others of a similar genre—has no magic power to make problems, poverty, or failures disappear on its own. It is a lantern to light up your footsteps while on the journey toward a better life. Happiness is a state of mind. Success is accessible to all, if you are willing to work at it to the best of your abilities. It is clear that all the institutions that are part of the society must play their part in alleviating human burdens, suffering, and poverty. But everyone has the duty to do his part. There is no exception. The command is simple: grow or die. I am confident you have chosen to grow.

So once again, what are you doing at this time? Is everything going as expected? If so, good luck and may it continue that way. If things are going otherwise, there is no more time to put it off. No more scapegoats and no more excuses. Make the decision now to come out of the rut. Take positive steps toward changing your situation. Screen your options, reorganize your priorities, choose your pathway, and you are on your way to success. If you err or fail, you can learn from previous missteps and move on. The key is to not remain static or stagnant. I have confidence that you can make the difference. I believe you and I share a common dream to see a better world, where everyone takes care of himself, his health, his finances, and his home; where the family's conditions will improve, the children are happy, obedient, and well-cared for. The difference is one person doing it one day at a time and doing the best he can under the circumstances. Sooner or later good will overcome evil. Let us start now. The sooner the better!

About the Author

Jean Daniel François received a B.S. in management in 1980, then an M.A. in economics in 1984. He worked in accounting and finance in a Fortune 500 company until 1986, when he decided to leave against all advice from others, who meant well, to go to New York Medical College, where he studied medicine and obtained his M.D. in 1992. Dr. François then went to SUNY Brooklyn, where he specialized in neurology and neurophysiology. While working in that field, he met the requirement to obtain a bachelor's degree, in theology, as well as an honorary doctorate in education in 2001. He is married and has two children.

Besides his medical practice, he founded in 1993 a community-based church where he currently holds the leadership position. Since his adolescence, his favorite pastimes have been reading, writing, and listening to music. He has written for a few community-based magazines and has been a conference speaker in the field of family counseling and domestic violence. He has served as the host of a weekly radio program that discusses various subjects for the advancement of underserved communities. Through his numerous articles, sermons, and conferences, he has always hoped to promote education, foster personal and community development, and help everyone get a better grasp on life. Dr. François wrote this book, *Prescription For A Successful Life*, based on his personal experience and readings. He hopes to promote change in all of his readers.

Proceeds from the sale of this book will help to cover the cost of publication and to foster his community activities, primarily based in Brooklyn, New York.

To order copies, visit your local bookstore.

To communicate your criticisms and comments, or to contact Dr. François about seminars and conference engagements, email JFRANC6704@AOL.COM or mail your letter to him at:

Jean Daniel François, M.D.
P.O. Box 360543, Brooklyn, NY 11236
Or call 718-531-6100, Fax: 718-531-2329.

Thank you!

Selected Resources

A complete list of the countless books I have read, documents I have seen, and correspondence I have received for the past several years would require a separate volume of references and bibliography. And even then, I would still run the risk of forgetting some people. Please accept the following incomplete list. I call upon the understanding and forgiveness of others, if I have inadvertently omitted a name. Thanks.

Albrektson, J. R.
Living Large
Colorado Springs, CO: Waterbrook Press, 2000

Bassham, Lanny
The Mental Management System With Winning in Mind
Portland, OR: BookPartners, Inc.,1988

Canfield, Jack
The Success Principles
New York, NY: Harper Collins Publishers, 2005

Hill, Napoleon
Think & Grow Rich
New York, NY: Random House Publishing Group, 1960

King, Larry
How to Talk to Anyone, Anytime, Anywhere:
The Secrets of Good Communication
New York, NY: Three Rivers Press, 1994

Lui, Meizhu, Barbara Robles, Betsy Leondar-Wright,
Rose Brewer and Rebecca Adamson
The Color of Wealth: The Story Behind the
U.S. Racial Wealth Divide
New York, NY: The New Press, 2006

Maxwell, John C.
*The 21 Indispensable Qualities of a Leader:
Becoming the Person Others Will Want to Follow*
Nashville, TN: Thomas Nelson, Inc., 1999

Mesiti, Pat
*Attitudes and Altitudes: the Principles, Practice and
Profile of Twenty-First Century Leadership*
NSW, Australia: Pat Mesiti Ministries, Inc., 1997

Moore, David. L., MD.
Your Best Way to Health
Atlanta, GA: Best Way to Health, Inc., 2000

Newberry, Tommy
Success Is Not an Accident
Woodlawn, TN: Looking Glass Books, 1997

Oliver, Melvin L. and Thomas M. Shapiro, eds.
*Black Wealth / White Wealth: A New Perspective on
Racial Inequality.* 2nd ed.
New York, NY: Routledge, 2006

Prosper, Jolene B.
Mind Your Own Business
Berrien Spring, MI: PTC Books, 2005

Self, Carolyn S. and Self, William L.
Survival Kit for Marriage
Nampa, ID: Pacific Press Publishing Association, 1998

Stanley, Charles F.
Living the Extraordinary Life
Nashville, TN: Thomas Nelson, Inc., 2005

Swindoll, Charles R.
Living Above the Level of Mediocrity
Nashville, TN: Thomas Nelson, Inc., 1987

Wheeler, Elmer
How to Sell Yourself to Others
New York, NY: Simon & Schuster, 1974

QUICK ORDER FORM

Email orders: **DRFRANCOISMD@GMAIL.COM**

Fax orders to: **718-531-2329**

Call for order at: **718-531-6100**
Have your credit card ready.

Mail in orders to:
    Jean D. François, MD
    P.O. Box 360543
    Brooklyn NY 11236

Please send the following Books, CD, Reports:

    I am interested in:

    ☐ Speaking/ seminars/conferences

    ☐ Consulting

    ☐ Other services needed: _____

Name: _____

Address: _____

City: _____State: _____ Zip: _____

Telephone: _____

Cell #: _____

Email address: _____

Shipping and handling:

    U.S: $5.00 for first book, $2.00 for each additional.

www.ingramcontent.com/pod-product-compliance
Lightning Source LLC
Chambersburg PA
CBHW050108280326
41933CB00010B/1015